To Lt Col David W. Fisher:
USMC - (once a marine 💙 always a Marine!)

Thank you sir for your service, self-less-ness - and bravery. I salute you - and wish you a healthy, wealthy, long + happy Life.

Lee A Shin
(LISA)

Never

Anticipate The Command

by Lee Summers

iUniverse, Inc.
Bloomington

Never Anticipate The Command

iUniverse books may be ordered through booksellers or by contacting:

iUniverse
1663 Liberty Drive
Bloomington, IN 47403
www.iuniverse.com
1-800-Authors (1-800-288-4677)

ISBN: 978-1-4620-6290-4 (sc)
ISBN: 978-1-4620-6291-1 (hc)
ISBN: 978-1-4620-6292-8 (e)

Library of Congress Control Number: 2011919359

Printed in the United States of America

iUniverse rev. date: 11/11/2011

To my father, my teacher, DI and best friend.

❧ INTRODUCTION ❧

My father was a marine, a combat staff sergeant who served in the South Pacific Theater during World War II. It was sometime during the second grade when I realized my home life was a bit different from the other little girls in school. When a classmate burst into tears over a hopscotch game, I looked on with disgust and said, "Champs don't cry! Snap out of it! Straighten up, soldier! Get a hold of yourself!"

I was quickly removed from the playground and marched down to the principal's office. All the while I stood in dismay, unaware of any wrongdoing on my part! Accused of being cruel and insensitive, a phone call home followed. I heard my mother's response to the call: "Oh, that's just her father talking! She's hard! She's just like him. She can be hard like a German."

At seven years old, my father punished me for ripping open a caterpillar cocoon with a stick. I had only done what the other kids in my neighborhood did in their leisure, when lucky enough to spot an intact cocoon. I thought nothing of it when my father assigned me to a "work party." I was to be, quote, "a single-man work party and rake the newly mowed grass clippings in our backyard, after he cut the lawn." It was hard labor, but I figured all the other kids on my block experienced similar disciplinary action. It wasn't until high school that I realized no one else complained about yard work or running laps around the block for punishment. I was shocked and jealous to hear my peers were only sent to their rooms. I would have loved that!

When all is said and done, however, having had a marine for a father shaped my life and personality and forged a steel discipline, physically and mentally unique to me. This mind-set emboldened me to win scholarships, perform as a concert pianist, compete on a swim team,

1

run marathons, and take care of beloved family members later on in life, when tragedy and illness struck.

At times, I can still hear my father's voice. It wasn't what he said, but also the *way* in which he said things. It was obvious that the Marine Corps not only shaped him, but in a particular way, it helped to heal him. When Dad was age six, my paternal grandfather died of a brain tumor, leaving a widow and four children: two sons and two daughters. The girls were older, and my dad was the third-born and elder son. Grandpa had given him "Champ" as a nickname. He was a professional boxer and had taught my dad boxing and how to win a fight. So at the tender age of six, with boxing lessons under his belt, a chip on his shoulder, and his dead father's coaching resonating in his ears, "Champs don't cry," my daddy faced the world alone. A penniless widow, my grandmother heard relatives request to take and raise three of her four children into different households. Two aunts wanted Janet and Fred, and an elder uncle Evelyn, but no one wanted my dad, Henry. He never forgot that day. Grandpa Gloverdanz put an end to the turmoil by announcing that his daughter, May, and the four kids would all live with him and Grandma Annie Carbury-Gloverdanz, that no one would be split up. He was lucky to have had such loving maternal grandparents; my dad always reflected, but the experience left deep scars.

When he joined the Corps, it became more than a way of life or a code of excellence. I believe the toughness and regimen acted as a fatherly force, strong and powerful and noble, which consumed him and helped him to forget.

That's why Hank was and will be a Marine forever, and remembered as such, first and foremost.

I can still hear him in my head: "C'mon! Get on with it already! Christ Almighty, snap out of your shit! No slackers here! I never crapped out! Straighten up and fly right! You don't know shit from beans!"

The verbiage goes on and on, and I guess it always will.

The silver lining in all this was my bedtime stories, however! I figured all children heard about Telagee and the "yaws," "Slug Marvin" and the garbage scow, K and C rations, Higgins boats, M1 rifles as comfort, and that malaria-carrying mosquitoes have zebra stripes. As my head hit the pillow, I strained to listen, to know everything my father had seen and felt! That many of the US troops would routinely play at dentistry to remove the gold fillings from dead Japanese soldiers. I can remember seeing the canopy, the green velvet of Bougainville jungles in my mind's eye. Even now, I know he watches over us, and I can hear his voice: "Good night, honey, sweet dreams! I love you!"

Chapter I

⟿ *1943* ⟾

If you threw a dart at a map in the dark while blindfolded and drunk, chances are, the mark you hit would have made for a better destination than Bougainville Island in 1943. The island weather was indescribably horrible! It rained every day for weeks straight—and not soft, gentle rain. It came down in torrents, pouring easily as Morton's salt. There wasn't a dry place to be had. The more it rained, the muddier the area became, until all you could see was a sea of rippling mud. Everywhere you walked, you were knee-deep in squishy, squashy mud. Our dungarees became heavy, and soggy cakes of mud hung on us like glue. Foxholes looked like bathtubs, always filled with water. Over 50 percent of the trucks were all bogged down in mud. These were replaced by tractors which pulled light trailer carts. These tractors sometimes took hours to go just a few miles. It was the only means of moving supplies to the front lines, however tedious.

But if the rain and mud hampered the marines, it must have frustrated the hell out of the Japs! Although they had forty-five thousand troops on this rock, they couldn't move the big guns through the mud. However, they did have a few 77s in action, which proved to be more harassing than effective. In fact, sometimes it was downright amusing! The Japs were zeroed in on a corned beef pile and hit it with amazing accuracy. The marines were never too keen on corned beef and chanted, "Hit it again! Hit it again, you bastards!" and the Japs complied for the rest of the night.

During this rainy spell, Captain Cantella received orders from superiors to move emergency rations "C" and "K" to an area called "Evansville." This was an advanced area, practically on the front line.

It was enemy territory. The object was to replenish the frontline troops with food supplies in case of an emergency. A working party from Dump #2 loaded a tractor-trailer cart with twenty-five cases of K rations and twenty-five cases of C rations. A group of four men, including Hank and the captain, left Dump #2 at approximately 1300 hours.

It was raining like hell, and the roads were in terrible shape. The tractor was operating in about two or three feet of mud. Everywhere you looked, vehicles were abandoned. Everything was stuck in the mud. The tractor driver had difficulty getting around some of the trucks, and boy, it was time-consuming! It took for-fucking-ever! After a while, the road started to narrow down until it became only a trail. It was called the "Numa Numa trail." The men sat on top of the boxes in the trailer cart. The captain rode on the tractor. Everyone was taking in the scenery—that is, if you could call it scenery! The trees were as thick as crabgrass, and you couldn't see five feet off the road. Green foliage blanketed the trees in all shapes and sizes. Small patches of fog created an eerie, spooky atmosphere. Even the noise of the tractor was swallowed up by its vastness.

Hank sat there in silence. All he could think was, *What a hellhole this rock is.* It had a surf as treacherous as a snake. They had lost Higgins boats to the terrain and the troops on them to strafings. Some men got hit climbing down the nets and fell into the boats with the packs still on their backs. His ship, the *Crescent City,* lost practically every Higgins boat coming in on the initially landing. The undertow was so strong that it could pull down a ship. The jungles were so thick with mangroves, trees, and foliage that you had to hack your way through it with a machete. The island contained massive, ugly swamps, infested with crocodiles, millions of foreign insects, three different types of malaria-carrying mosquitoes, and rats big as cats to contend with that nibbled on your toes and fingers while you were asleep. The land crabs were as big as lobsters and scorpions were almost a foot long. Bougainville had land snakes, water snakes, two-legged snakes (what we called the Japs), cannibalistic native tribes, an active volcano, earthquakes, air raids night and day (take your pick!), shellings, a hot bastard sun, torrential rains, mud, fog, bombings, and strafings! The only thing left were piss and punk. The Hawk was right when he said, "A guy could develop a nervous condition here beginning right in his asshole."

As they continued along at a snail's pace, the scenery became more interesting. Jap bodies were lying everywhere, some with no heads, others with no legs or arms. This was a sobering part of the tour. Everyone was alert now and, believe it or not, enjoying it thoroughly. The Hawk was having a ball. Standing high on the boxes, he would shout, "Wait till you see this bastard," or "Get a look at this son of a bitch." Then he would holler, "There's a beaut coming up on the starboard side." As we came abreast of the scene, about fifteen giant-size rats were ripping a man apart. Someone remarked that he must be an officer because they were eating him first. "If he is," the Hawk replied, "they'll end up with indigestion for sure."

To a civilian, this kind of talk sounds vulgar and barbaric, but to a marine in combat, it is therapeutic. He has been indoctrinated thoroughly. The enemy loses his identity as a man. He is no longer a man; he is a thing, a thing that is hated, hunted, and destroyed. At that moment, the Japs controlled three airfields on the island: Kara, Kahili, and Buka. The Japanese bombed and strafed the troops with planes that came from the island of Rabaul. The condition of this island was *black*, which meant that the outcome of the island was in doubt. Everyone was aware that the Japanese Navy was on its way there to shell the marines and would try to land troops to destroy the Americans. Hank was thinking to himself, *So if our navy does not intercept them at sea, then the island will become a marine graveyard—my graveyard.* That was a reality never too far from a soldier's mind. However, at that moment, despite the hardships, there wasn't the slightest doubt in any man's mind about who would lose the island! From the lowest-ranking marine to the highest-ranking officer, every marine was indoctrinated, Hank reflected. Each marine believed that he was the best fighting military man in the world, barring any foreign power. For this belief he would fight and, if necessary, die like a marine.

The noise of machine-gun fire became louder as the journey continued. Gunfire makes a person pick up his ears like a police dog. It also makes your eyes shift nervously. The swoosh of artillery fire alerts your senses differently. You strain your ears and tilt your head then think intently. "Was the last sound from the right ear or the left one? In other words, is it coming or going?" The bullets swooshing over their heads seemed to be going. That somewhat eased the minds of the soldiers in the trailers.

They had been traveling two hours now but had not covered much territory. The mud was bad, but the rain was worse. The men's dungarees were soaked, and the group was chilled to the bone. Suddenly, they turned off the road, and they were going in and following a little path through the jungle. They continued on for over a half mile. The jungle was thick and ghostly looking. In a small clearing, about a hundred yards from a river, they stopped. The captain said, "This is good enough." They unloaded the boxes into four piles. Afterward, they started to explore the area.

In the woods behind the clearing, they came upon a few dead Japanese. They examined them carefully and figured that they couldn't have been dead too long, for the wounds and blood looked fresh. One Jap must have been hit by a mortar shell. He was decapitated, and half of his chest lay exposed. The only thing that Hank could have likened it to was a bee's honeycomb. The Hawk insisted it looked more like a giant Chinese apple. In front of them was a body of water. They examined that too. It was crystal clear, and they could see fish swimming in it. They were knee-deep in mud now, and the rain continued to pour down.

Finally, the captain gave the order to board the trailer. When they were all aboard, he turned around and said, "Hank, you stay here with the rations. We'll be back with another load, and we'll pick you up then."

Hank estimated that by the time they got back to Dump #2, it would be almost dark. Who the hell would ride these trails at night? Hank knew the answer to that, "No one!"

The Hawk must have been reading Hank's mind, for he asked the captain if he could also remain. "No," the captain replied. "You'll be all right, won't you, Corporal?"

"Yes, sir," came the reply.

The captain grinned. "Don't let anyone steal those rations."

"Don't worry about that, Captain," snapped Hank. "The only ones who know it's here are me and the dead Japs, and they're not eating anymore."

Rocky, to be smart, shouted, "And you might not be eating anymore after tonight either! But don't worry about a thing, kid. I'll take care of all your girlfriends. I'll visit your mother and tell her how you protected those rations. I told you once before that those C rations will kill you one way or another!"

Hank was burning. "Laugh, you lard-ass bastard! I hope ya hit a mine on the way back. But don't worry, I'll find your fat ass tomorrow and I'll bury you, and then I'll piss on your grave for luck!"

And so it concluded. Soon they were out of Hank's sight, and the silence of the jungle became deafening.

Hank sat on top of the C rations. The rain was coming down in torrents. He was wet, cold, and miserable. And very lonely. Suddenly, he couldn't control himself any longer and shouted at the top of his lungs, "You no-good asshole captain! You no-good fucking son of a bitch! I hate your fucking guts, and I hope they shoot you right in your fucking ass! God damn you!"

Then Hank saw something move in the woods. He quickly jumped off the boxes and ran back to the woods with the dead Japs and hid behind a tree. He figured if it was Japs, they would head straight for the boxes.

Out of the woods came one lone figure. It spoke, "Hey! Anybody around here?"

Hank practically flew out of the woods. "Where did you come from?" he excitedly asked. "Boy, am I glad to see you! What are you doing here?" Hank inquired.

The marine explained, "I'm on my way to sick bay; I was bitten on the hand by a scorpion."

Hank looked at his hand. It was swollen up like a balloon. "Does it hurt?"

"Are you kidding?" came the answer. "When that bastard bit me, it was like a mule kicked me. It blew up right away and numbed my whole arm. Right now I'm sick to my stomach." The guy grimaced in pain and asked, "Can you tell me where sick bay is?"

Hank wished he could help but told him that he had only arrived there less than an hour ago himself. "My captain left me here to watch these fucking rations."

As sick as the boy was, a grin came to his face. "You're kidding. Who the hell would want to steal C rations? Why, even the fucking Japs don't want them." Many times during the still of the night, a Jap would holler out, "Ma-lines eat C rations; Ma-lines eat shit!"

Hank laughed as the marine turned to leave. "Gee, I'm sorry I can't help you. I know there's a sick bay near Dump #2, about a mile and a half from here, but you'd have to walk in mud up to your ass."

"Thanks, buddy, but I had enough of that shit! There must be one close by," said the soldier. He waved good-bye to Hank and said, "Nice talking to you." Then in the next breath, the soldier shouted, "Hey, are you planning on spending the night here? If you are, you're nuts! There's only Japs in front of you! My outfit is dug in about a half mile to your right. We made contact with the Japs three times today, but tonight they'll contact us. You can bet your ass on it! So if you want to get to our lines, you better go now while it's still light. Don't try going at dusk. Our orders are to shoot anything that walks! Besides, we have a lot of trigger-happy bastards who will shoot your ass full of holes." He waved again and took off.

For the rest of the afternoon, Hank did nothing but sit on a box and stare out into the boondocks. He thought about home, girls, his mother, brother and sisters, basketball, football, baseball, and tennis. The rain continued to pour down, and Hank practically relived his whole life. It is amazing what memories can do for a lonely person. Happy memories keep you rational. He could hear the football signals in games in which he had played. In fact, he relived every sporting event in which he had participated. He could see faces. Then his mind turned to parties he had attended. He remembered the girls, the office parties, New York on a New Year's Eve, and summers at the beach. There were smiles and laughter, tears and frowns. He could see his mother's Sunday dinners. He could even smell the food.

At this, he jumped up. "Hell, man, I'm hungry!" he snapped. He picked up a tripod that he had in his pocket along with the heat tabs. He lighted them quickly, and they glowed with a blue flame. He broke open a can of C rations; it was stew. He placed that on the tripod and in no time at all, it was boiling. He rearranged the ration boxes and made a shelter. He felt cozy sitting there listening to the rain beat down on the boxes. He caught some rainwater in his canteen cup and added a little of it to the beef stew. Inhaling deeply, it gave off the aroma of a Thanksgiving turkey. He tasted it. It was a delicious meal, one that he would never forget. He heated a canteen of water and made cocoa. That, too, hit the spot. He sat back, lit a cigarette, and blew the smoke out into the dimly lit, foggy atmosphere. He was still wet and cold but not quite as miserable. The hot stew gave him the pickup he needed.

Hank realized it was getting dark. He knew the captain would not be back tonight. Despite his doubts, he kept telling himself they would return. They would! They would! They wouldn't leave him here alone. They just wouldn't! Hell, they couldn't! Well, he figured he would prepare anyhow, just in case. He checked his M1 rifle. It was a comfort and one of the few sources of consolation he had. The other was his St. Anthony statue. He kept it in his pocket over his heart. The face was worn smooth, and the finish rubbed off the wood. Like his dog tags, the statue was always on him. At times, in his loneliness, he would talk to the saint. It seemed he could hear the saint answering him, reassuring him in his soft, comforting words that "Yes, everything will be all right, you'll see." He put on his cartridge belt containing fifty rounds of ammunition, gathered two bandoliers of ammo, and placed them at his feet. He also had two hand grenades by his side. In his heart, Hank sincerely hoped that he wouldn't have to use anything.

In the pitch blackness of the night, Hank sat in the makeshift shelter. His rifle was slung over his knee, and the constant pitter-patter of rain beat down heavily on the boxes. Occasionally, rainwater would splash on his face. He stared aimlessly out into the darkness, straining his eyes for moving figures or listening intently for strange noises.

All of a sudden, his pulse quickened. He heard a distinct noise coming from his right side. He listened again. There was no mistaking it. He could hear boots sloshing in the mud. Nervously, his index finger played with the trigger of his M1 rifle.

"Where are you? Where are you? You C-ration commando, where are you?"

Hank recognized the voice as the marine who had gone to sick bay. He poked his head out of the shelter while at the same time lighting his Zippo lighter. He hollered, "Over here, over here." Hank's morale went up 100 percent. "How did you make out?"

The boy shook his head. "I never found the goddamn place." He sat down on a box, took off his helmet, and shook his head from side to side. "Wow, I'm soaking wet. You know, I've been wandering round in circles for hours. There's nothing out there. It's spooky, believe me, I was scared out of my ass! Then I found the river and just kept following it. Once I went down in the mud up to my ass. Another time I fell flat on my face in the mud. A couple of times I thought I saw men, but it was my imagination." He put his hand on his chest. "My heart is still pounding like a drum! It was just by accident that I found you, and boy, am I glad!" He grimaced in pain. "God! My hand hurts like hell, and my head. God, am I sick!" He started to heave, and his body quivered and shook convulsively. He had the chills and moaned continually.

Hank didn't know what to do. He asked the boy if he could make him a cup of hot cocoa or some C-ration stew. He received a snotty reply. "Stick the C ration up your ass and piss on your Ks."

Hank realized then the soldier had a high fever. Hank handed him a canteen of water, which he threw out into the blackness. "I told you I don't want a goddamn thing." The guy then started rattling on about the sergeants, saying it was all their fault, and the officers, the Japs, the war, his home. He asked for a butt. Hank gave him one. He lit it and took one long drag and continued to light a Zippo lighter which had a flame like a blowtorch.

"Hey, knock that shit off!" shouted Hank. "What do you wanna do, bring the goddamn Japs down on us?"

"Piss on them. Who cares. Up their ass!"

"Listen, this is my hole," Hank shouted. "And if you don't like it, then get the hell out!"

"Make me!" he answered.

Hank looked at him with daggers in his eyes. At this point, he didn't know whom he hated more, the Japs or this obnoxious bastard. But he acted fast. "Look, shithead, I don't want any trouble from you. You're a snotty, fucking bastard, and you're not getting any more cigarettes! Now knock off that Zippo shit or I'll knock this shack down, and both our asses will be out in the rain!"

"Go ahead, I'm not interested," the marine said, continuing to ignite the Zippo.

Hank looked at him for a while. Then saying in a loud voice, "I have had enough of this shit!" he kicked and pushed the two sides down, not caring if they fell on the marine or not. When it was all over, the marine was still sitting there. Hank grabbed a couple of boxes. He put them near a tree about thirty feet from the broken ration pile. Hank sat on the boxes and used the trunk of a tree as a back rest. Again, he placed his rifle over his knee and his ammo at his feet. He sat back and prepared for a miserable night.

The rain kept coming down in a steady pour. Hank kept looking out into the pitch blackness. He was soaked, but at least he had the satisfaction of knowing his buddy couldn't use the lighter. Every once in a while, he would doze off. But the rain hitting his face made sure he didn't take more than five.

Suddenly he woke up with a start. "I see you, I see you, you son of a bitch; I know you're out there!" the marine was screaming. Then, *crack-crack-crack*; three shots rang out!

Hank was on his feet in a second and made his way to the marine in front of him. Hank whispered, "Where are they? I heard them too."

"I figure about a hundred fifty feet. I think they're near that brook."

"Look," said Hank, "let's go into the jungle in back of us. Please let's go and don't shoot. Goddamn it, don't shoot! We'll lie on the ground near the tree where I was before. I'm sure if we don't give away our position, they won't find us. Perhaps they'll go away."

"I'm scared," said the marine.

"So am I, but don't shoot, Christ almighty! Please don't shoot!"

Slowly and quietly, the two made their way back into the woods. Crawling on their elbows in a prone position in the mud like a snake was difficult, but they made it. Now they were side by side, straining their eyes to see out into pitch blackness. Hank remembered then what his DI had said back in boot camp: "When it's black out there and you're alone and scared, try to keep your composure by remembering this. You can see anything you want to—a boat, a house, a man, a dog, etc." He tried it and sure enough, he could. It made him feel just a little better.

He whispered to the marine, "How are you feeling?"

"Lousy, my head is killing me. God, it's buzzing like hell, and I'm scared, real scared. I'm sorry about what happened before."

"Forget it. Hey, by the way, my name is Hank."

"And mine is Steve. Boy, isn't this some shit. Now I can feel the water trickling down my neck."

They lay there for about twenty minutes when the crack of a Jap 25 startled them. Again and again it went off. The men were straining their ears. Steve was right; it was by the stream about a hundred or more yards to their left. The Japs were waiting for return fire and when it didn't come, they sprayed the woods with rifle fire. A couple of bullets ricocheted off the trees, and the marines could hear the whine as they plopped into the mud. "I'm getting out of here," whispered Steve.

"Shut up," whispered Hank. "They can't see us. Just shut the hell up."

Everything was quiet again. Five, ten minutes went by, and Steve just up and left. A few minutes after that, the Jap rifle fire began again, and Hank was more scared than ever. Now he could hear Steve's voice ring out. "Up your ass, you sons of bitches, you yellow fucks!" After that, there were five consecutive shots from an M1 rifle. "They're over here, Hank! Over here! Here!" His voice seemed to be coming from Hank's left. Another volley of shots rang out, followed by a sickening cry. "Hank! Oh my God!"

Without thinking, Hank sprang to his feet and ran as fast as he could in the direction of the stream. He was about thirty or forty feet from the stream when he again heard and saw flashes of light from the Japs' rifles. Quickly, he hit the deck and slid into a foot of muck and mud. He grabbed a grenade, pulled the pin, and tossed it in the direction of the gunfire. He took his second grenade and did the same thing. As soon as it exploded, he ran another ten feet. At the same time he hit the deck, he emptied eight shots in that direction. Putting another clip into his rifle, he waited, and waited, and waited.

Everything was so quiet now. The rain came down in torrents. He could feel the water and slimy mud ooze into his dungarees. It was cold, but he was too afraid to move. He prayed to St. Anthony.

As time went on, he became more miserable but he dared not move. He lay there with his head down in the mud. He clenched his rifle. It was ready to bark at any noise, but there was only a ghostly silence.

Then it started to get light, and the fear of being discovered gripped Hank again. The lighter it became, the more frightened he too became. *I don't mind dying,* he thought, *but not like this, not here, not in this shithole! Not like this, for Christ's sake.* He reached for St. Anthony in his pocket, and the well-worn lines in the carved wooden figure soothed the soldier immediately. He could hear the voice. The saint was saying, "No, not here, son. Not today, don't worry. Everything will be okay. I promise, it will all turn out okay. I promise. You'll live to a ripe old age with your loved ones around you, in comfort and in warmth. It will be okay," said the voice, and Hank hung on every word. "God help me," he prayed.

It was still raining and pockets of fog clustered near the stream, rising like smoke from a smoldering fire. Finally, he stood up. He was numb with cold as he surveyed the area cautiously. He ran for the nearest tree and took cover behind a large tree trunk. He peeked out, looking toward the river. There, in a gully by the stream, lay two Japs. Hank froze. Holding his breath, he could hear his pulse quicken. He held his rifle at parade dress, ready to shoot from the left or right.

It seemed like he had been standing there for an hour. In reality, only a few minutes had passed. He tilted his head and strained his ears, but heard only the steady pitter-patter of raindrops hitting the leaves and plopping into mud. It seemed to echo over and over in his mind. He looked above. In the dismal gloomy atmosphere, he didn't see or hear a bird.

He decided to take second peek. The two Japs were still lying there. He watched them for a few moments. With his rifle at the ready, he moved closer and closer. Then he spotted four more Japs. They were lying half in and half out of the water. He could see blood on one of them. He thought perhaps they were only wounded. He would have shot them all again except he was afraid that the noise of the gunfire would surely bring someone to the area. He picked up a rock and let it roll down into the gully. No one moved. He threw two more before he was satisfied that all the enemy troops were dead.

Lowering himself down into the gully, Hank was amazed at the amount of spent cartridge shells. The place was littered with them. Examining the dead nips, he noticed that none of them wore a helmet. Their wounds also looked superficial. They appeared asleep, and any minute he was half-expecting them to wake up, shouting and screaming. He walked around the area looking for Steve. He thought to himself, *Where the hell could he have gone?* When he couldn't find him, he figured perhaps he went back to his outfit. But if he did, Hank wondered, wouldn't he have brought help? On second thought, for one man—Hell no! One man was expendable. No one would have come.

He drifted back to the dead Japs. Then something caught his eye. One of the dead men wore a raincoat. Perhaps he was an officer. Hank turned him over. His face was a bloody mess. A piece of shrapnel had torn right into his skull. Hank removed the raincoat, thinking all the time, *This poor bastard won't be needing it anymore.* He tried it on. "Not bad, a little tight, a little short, but who gives a shit! It's a nice color and it's light. It also has a detachable hood." Suddenly, Hank remembered today was his birthday. His twenty-third birthday. He thought for a moment. Looking down at the dead Jap, he said, "Thank you for the birthday present, you poor son of a bitch."

He walked on and, although the rain was still coming down, it seemed to lighten up. He restacked the boxes of rations and sat inside, waiting for the captain to return. It was so very quiet. He thought about the events of the preceding evening. *How ironic,* he thought. *The only present I get is from an enemy soldier. But I was left here alone like a sitting duck by my captain! He's still sore over a few cases of beer that I didn't even take!* Hank thought. *If I ever get off this piss-and-punk rock, I am going to remember this poncho, a terrific birthday present, and the unlucky soul who offered it to me. At least* his *misery is over now.*

It was a night he would always remember and a birthday he would have liked to forget.

* * *

"Oh, Dad! That was awful! No party? No cake? Not even a card?" I asked. "Tell me more, Dad," I begged. "Weren't you afraid?"

"Well, yes, I was," he answered.

"Can you tell me the location again?" I asked. I ran to find a pen and paper and he laughed at me, a white-toothed, handsome grin.

"You know I'm writing a book, honey," he added.

"Yeah, but you never finish it!" I snapped.

"Well, maybe you can help me with that. It's your job now—you can finish the book. You be the writer."

Somewhere in the late 1970s, his deep blue-green eyes shone on me, and after kissing me goodnight, he tousled my hair, folded his big, strong arms, and sat upright, revealing broad, strong shoulders. The marine physique never left, because he exercised daily. "I'm starting to think you mean business about the book," he said.

"You bet I do, Dad," I shot back.

"Okay—then we must start at the beginning."

So my dear reader, here it is, from the beginning.

CHAPTER II

⊰ *1942* ⊱

On September 1, 1939, the day Adolf Hitler invaded Poland, the Marine Corps numbered 19,705 officers and men, less than what would later be known as a "reinforced division." Without aid of the draft, the Marine Corps increased in strength to slightly less than 100,000 men by the first week of February 1942.[1] Jack Mulligan, Jimmy Beaumont, and myself enlisted in February 1942. Because of the crowded conditions, they took us in dribs and drabs. Beaumont was called in April and Jack in April. I received a letter from Jack saying that they would be leaving Parris Island by June 15, 1942. Both would go to school in Quantico, Virginia, at the Marine Air Corps' school.

June 1, 1942 came and went, and I found myself in the waiting position. Ma kept telling me, "Don't worry, they will take you soon enough," but I couldn't be patient. I was straining at the bit. Every day someone else would leave for the service. Frankie M. joined the Army Air Corps, Rabbit was in the Merchant Marine, Joe F. joined the navy, Eddie and Lee were in Fort Dix, and Bill was at Fort Bragg. Each of these fellows had asked me to join with them. Some had even begged me. We were so close. We grew up together, played ball together, etc. Our lives, once entwined so closely, would never be the same. Of the fifty friends who served, I saw only five again. I think that was it. A lot were killed, but the majority of them returned to civilian life, and our paths would never cross again.

By this time, I was too concerned to worry about anything other than joining the Marine Corps. Work was okay, but I wasn't interested.

---

1 Aurthur RA, Cohlmia K. RT Vance, Ed. (1948) *The Third Marine Division.* Washington, DC: Infantry Journal Press.

I ran on autopilot. I was nineteen years old and raring to go. I was never afraid of being drafted but wanted no part of the army. Not that I had anything against the army, but my heart was set on being a marine, and a marine I was going to be. Come hell or high water. I had made up my mind.

Physically, I conditioned myself with all sorts of exercise. Every day I spent one or two hours on physical conditioning. Tuesday and Thursday evenings, my brother and I would work out at the YMCA. We would start off with exercises and end up with twenty or thirty men following us. I believe they thought we were instructors. We would end with a mile run and a good swim, and finish up at the Borden Bowl on Broad and Market streets in Newark. A jumbo hot fudge sundae for twenty cents would kill the night. After a while of performing this regimen, I felt like I could walk through doors, locked doors, steel doors.

I decided that night it was time to assert myself. After all, it couldn't do any harm, and I was on salary. I'd get paid for the day anyhow.

At nine o'clock, June 2, 1942, I reported to the Marines Recruiting Station, located in the basement of the Newark City Hall. Sergeant Bloy extended me a cordial welcome; it wasn't our first meeting. He knew well the information I wanted, "When am I reporting for duty?"

"Sorry, kid, can't help you," he replied.

Sergeant Bloy had a smirk that irked me. I studied him closely. He was pudgy. *When I'm a marine, I'm not going to be like that*, I thought to myself. The place was crowded with young men, some wanting to join, others just curious. Large posters in the hallway reflected on the young faces. It sometimes influenced their decision to join a certain branch of the service, such as "Join the marines, a fighting man's outfit," "Join the army, the backbone of America's might" or "Join the navy, see the world, plus action."

Stepping out into the hallway, a navy recruiter also recognized me. "Hi there, bucko. Still waiting to get into that bellhop outfit?" he hollered.

"Yep," I replied.

The navy recruiter continued, "Frig them *gyrenes*! Join a good outfit! By the time they take you, the war will be over!" He kept making waves. "Join the navy today, go next week—no waiting." He had gathered quite an audience, and Marine Sergeant Bloy was out there too. I was observing him.

Bloy came over to me and invited me into his office. He picked up the phone and said in a commanding voice, "Sit down, boy," while talking to his party. "You still want to go?" he questioned.

"Yes, sir," I replied.

He hung up the phone and turned to me. "You're leaving from here tomorrow. Be here at 7:30 a.m. sharp. Get that, boy? Seven thirty a.m. sharp!"

The words were still sinking in when I left the room. Once outside, I took a deep breath. The navy recruiter saw me. He was grinning. In a sarcastic voice, he stated, "You'll be sorry, boy. You'll be sorry!"

The day flew by. I went to New York, to my office where I worked. Saying good-bye wasn't easy. I had many happy memories there, so many. I had lunch with Mrs. I. J. Francisco and Mr. R. Holiday. They were such wonderful people and faithfully wrote me once a week the entire time I was away. They were always sending me something, everything from money to cookies. They bought me gifts from every department: a grooming set, pen and pencil sets, razors, writing paper, money belt, wallet, bottles of scotch, gin, rye, cigarettes by the carton, and an envelope with fifty dollars in it. There is also another envelope with forty dollars from the Examiners' Department. All in all, I made a good haul. There were so many guys and gals to thank, that it took me the rest of the day to get around to everyone. These were New Yorkers and they were something again! The best!

And the girls … In a building that's twenty-five stories high, you get to meet an awful lot of people. I was so interested in one girl, however, that I never had any time for the others. When that affair ended, I guess everybody knew it in old New York. I never took advantage of the situation, and rebounding wasn't my way. I received eighty letters a week from these gals, and I answered every one. They did keep my morale up as well as my ego.

When I returned home, my mother was sad, but there were no tears. I had called her earlier and gave her the news. There was no shock. I requested fried chicken for my last dinner at home. My mother had it piled on a platter like a mountain, and she was some cook! That night our family was together. We laughed and joked about things that happened years ago. The long years—we talked of the happy times, the sad times, about my father, my grandparents, friends, the year Louie's Cocktail Lounge gave Janet a bottle of champagne to give to the priest of our parish, Father Whitikemp, but instead, we decided to drink it. I, Janet, Evelyn, Fred, whoever was there, helped to finish it. It was good! We had a hearty laugh over that!

My mother had barely cleaned the dishes off the table when the doorbell rang. We had not planned anything special for this evening. All I wanted was a nice quiet night, a night to relax, to think, and talk to my family—my mother, my sisters, and my brother. This was not meant to be, however. At the door, there were friends, relatives, and neighbors. The Mulligans and the Manfriedos, the Rileys, the Bocages, the Bocks, the Riccas, the Mililos, and the Heneberrys! Also, the Stickels, the Krafts, and the Fletchers. And then girlfriends and boyfriends began to arrive. High school friends stopped, and CYO friends dropped in. Before you knew it, our home was overflowing with people; over seventy people showed up, and more were still arriving.

My uncle Charlie and Mr. Mulligan went to the store and bought quarts of beer and a few bottles of whiskey. More friends went out and bought popcorn, pretzels, rolls, cold cuts, salads, etc. In no time at all, we had a full-blown party going.

I received gifts galore: pen and pencil sets, money and money belts, cartons of cigarettes, Ronson and Zippo lighters, a wristwatch, military sets, even prayer books, rosaries, a statue of St. Anthony, and blessed medals. At the party, the conversations were light and the laughter was hearty. We reminisced and sang songs. Gaiety and good feelings prevailed throughout the evening.

All good things must come to an end, and our party started breaking up after midnight. However, it wasn't until after 2:00 a.m. that the last person left. The majority of these people I would never see again. I didn't know they were walking out of my life forever, and at the time, I had such a beautiful, warm feeling.

The memories of this occasion would linger on and on. So much so that the embers never died; they linger still. There, stacked on tiny shelves in the corner of my brain, they remain, and in moments of solitude, while on a train, in a car, almost anywhere. They flash back and once again I see the smiling, happy faces of dear ones, friends and relatives alike, coming to pay homage to a young man. A young man who was ever so grateful, but who had enough reserve as to never let his emotions betray him. Just to think that these people remembered and thought enough of me to see me off for war without even being asked was enough, but the presents they brought and the good feelings they expressed were amazing.

How could I forget the laughter and the tears, the emotional well-ups in their eyes as they bade me farewell, Godspeed, good luck, and "till we meet again." With people such as these, it is easy to remember and so hard to forget. The memory lasted my lifetime.

Later, lying in my bed with my arms folded under my head, I thought of all the good things that happened over the years. My brother's snoring didn't even bother me tonight. It was so comfortable here. My mother had made it so homey, with new twin beds and a new rug. I was seeing things for the first time. This was such a spacious room. Funny I hadn't noticed it before. My last day home, and I finally became aware of the things around me. Our king-size bathroom with the stall shower and a large bathtub was beautiful. How I loved to take showers! Yes, I would miss all of these things. Now I had reservations about leaving. Perhaps I was too hasty, but turning back the clock wouldn't help. I had made my decision. This was it. I brushed the thoughts from my head.

My mind wandered to the future. I wondered how the new life would be. I knew I would adapt to the Marine Corps, but how long would it take, the adjustment period? My mind wandered again. Boys and men have a certain thing about food. I had read in the papers that the food in the service was lousy. Perhaps it was only the army, not the marines. A thought entered my head: *God, I'm going to miss my Ma's cooking.* Reflecting on her past meals, I knew that she was the best cook in the whole world. Yes, "Mary Small" and her "small piano," the spinet in the parlor, would be sorely missed by this elder son!

My mind continued to travel about the night's activities. I never realized how nice Lenore and Barbara were. Here were two good-looking "heads," and I had been promising to take them out for well over a year. It would have to wait. How stupid of me. They were real nice girls. And God! The shape on Barbara—she looked like a young Rita Hayworth, and her attributes were many. When we were growing up, my friends and I would classify girls with our own standards. This was no reflection on a girl's personality but strictly on their looks. We would put them into categories according to ship sizes like PT boats, destroyers, cruisers, and battleships. I preferred destroyers and cruisers, and I considered Lenore a sleek destroyer. Barbara was definitely a light cruiser. Both of them had guns with plenty of firepower!

Five full months had passed since my experience with Moon, "my true love." I gave her the nickname Moon after the comic strip, and she loved it. God, where does the time go? I was coming out of my shell slowly but surely. The ordeal left its mark, but not in a nasty way. I wasn't bitter. How could I be? On the contrary, it was a wonderful, warm experience. It was a time for growing up, and to me it would always be an unforgettable remembrance. My first true love. She was married now, and well, time is a great healer. I often wondered if she ever thought of me.

Something popped into my head; I remembered something. I hopped out of bed with a great leap and rushed to my dresser. I drew open the bottom drawer and in the dimly lit room, started fumbling and looking for a prized possession. Groping with my hands, I found it. There it was, just as I had placed it months ago. Quickly, I pulled it out and laid the bundle on my bed. Swiftly, I untied the package and placed everything in neat order and according to the proper perspective. First the gold kerchief, then the light-blue bra, the matching panties, the dark sheer nylon stockings, winter-white blouse, jacket, and matching skirt. The high-heeled patent-leather shoes finished it off. Her outfit from Christmas Eve. Everything was there, just as I had left it, including the rouge and the lipstick. It was the only gift I ever asked her for. I recalled the surprised look on her face. "You want what?"

"Your outfit—the clothes you are wearing tonight! I want to remember you just like this! Even the makeup you're forever fussing with!" I said. She had obliged.

I stood there gazing down at the items on the bed, thinking deeply, just staring, looking with a heartfelt reverence. The faint smell of perfume drifted through the room, penetrating my nostrils. Deeply, I inhaled its delicate fragrance, stirring my imagination even more. I could almost feel her presence. I missed her, and knew I would always love her.

My brother's second round of snores quickly jolted me back to reality. Slowly, gently, I folded each garment neatly and placed them back in my bureau drawer. Yes, my drawer of secrets. I took one final look and closed the drawer. There they would remain until I returned from war.

It was a long, long night. I turned out the light and flopped into my bed. Tomorrow would be an exciting day. Of that I was certain.

CHAPTER III

Time is a strange thing. It has so many unbelievable effects. When you're expecting something important to happen, it moves slowly. When you're having a good time, it moves quickly. The morning that I was being inducted into the Marine Corps, it was flying. Like a blur, it just flew!

At six o'clock in the morning, my mother had breakfast on the table. Hotcakes and sausages with Log Cabin maple syrup were waiting for me. This was my favorite breakfast and she knew it. Breakfast in our house, any day, any year, was a pleasant experience. I can truthfully say that in our house everyone started the day with a smile, and this day was no different. My brother was in good humor—dry, corny, but he could make you laugh. My sisters were exceptionally jovial that morning, and my mother, who bore the brunt of most of our jokes, enjoyed the fanfare. Her good-naturedness was definitely shining through on this particular day.

As a family, we were always concerned about one another. That's how we survived. When the going was rough, we met every obstacle head-on and always looked to the bright side. Going to war was no different. It was something that needed to be done. We would do it and survive with no tears. There were no tears as I kissed them good-bye at the door. We were never ones to look back.

They insisted on seeing me off at Penn Station. I told them if I could, I would let them know where I was leaving from. And so, with a smile on my face and a lump in my throat, I boarded the bus for downtown Newark and waved good-bye. I recognized familiar faces of everyday travelers. Yes, the same profiles, the young, the old. People going to work, to school—these were the commuters. No one ever spoke on this bus, or at least I never saw them speak, yet they communicated with each other in some form or manner, either by a nod of the head, a wink, a raised eyebrow, or a twist of the finger. Any one of these salutations was a recognition, an acknowledgment.

It was like any ordinary workday, except that I would not return home that evening. In my seat, gazing out the window, contemplating the day, I couldn't help but notice tiny sunbeams floating in and out of the open windows, some remaining and hitching a free ride to downtown Newark. It was a beautiful day, typical late-spring day, and I felt as springy as the weather. Inside me there was a tingling, the sort of thing you feel before a ball game or before a fight, but outside I felt good. I felt terrific. I had on my good slacks, a new sport shirt, and a lightweight sports jacket. Whenever dressed up, I felt good; it added to my ego. This was a real ego-driven day.

The bus neared my stop, and I prepared to pull the buzzer cord. Suddenly I realized that I held a shoebox on my lap. My mother handed me the box as I left. I knew it was chock full of goodies, but in the excitement, I forgot to thank her. I accepted it unconsciously. The sheer weight of the box caught my attention now. *Good God, there must be weights in here*, I thought to myself, getting off the bus.

The marine sergeant was awaiting our arrival at the recruiting station, as two of us walked through the door. We heard him holler to the doctor, "That's it, doc, that makes eight. Start running them through!" Eight of us were leaving this morning for Parris Island, South Carolina. The doctor gave us a quick physical checkup, and the recruiting sergeant handed each of us a sealed envelope. In no time at all, we were headed for Penn Station.

As we entered Penn Station, Newark, New Jersey, I couldn't help but think of so many memories. So many events over the years all started here. To name a few, trips to the Jersey shore: Asbury Park, Bradley Beach, Belmar, Spring Lake, Atlantic City. Trips taken to New York, to see the ball games, the Yankees, the Dodgers, the Giants, the big-name bands, Glen Island Casino, the dates, the girls, the work, my job. In retrospect, everything that started here had turned out pretty well. That was a good omen, something to think about. I held onto that thought.

The ride to New York City was uneventful. Once there, we were pushed along by the tide of people as we exited onto Courtland Street in downtown Manhattan. The Marine Corps recruiting office was located on Broadway, a short distance from the tube station. The short walk was invigorating and afforded you a last opportunity to see the large masses of people hustling and bustling to their jobs, walking in the streets, zigzagging, jaywalking in all directions, paying little or no attention to the honking horns and irritating drivers. Their only concern was getting to work. They knew exactly where to go and slowly disappeared into mountains of buildings surrounding this hub. I loved watching these people and their mannerisms. It was fascinating, to say the least. This was New York.

The marine recruiting station in New York City wasn't anything to write home about. It was a dingy, dirty building located right in the heart of downtown. It gave me a depressed feeling right from the start. I looked at the number halfheartedly and walked into the building, examining the archaic structure, thinking to myself, *Is this it?* Doing a complete about-face, I walked out. Again, I looked up at the number, disappointed as I was. The address was correct—this was it. Wandering into a dimly lit hallway without asking any questions, I saw the sign Marine Recruiting Station 2nd Floor. With this kind of advertisement, I didn't figure they could even attract Boy Scouts.

Once inside, marines moved us along rapidly and in an orderly fashion. Thirty new recruits were being processed this morning. We received two physical examinations, the first under normal conditions, the second after performing strenuous exercise. We went in and out of doors, seeing one doctor, then another, for a solid hour. By the time they had finished with us, the magic number was down to twenty-one men. Nine recruits were turned down, rejected for something or another. I felt pity for these young men. They wanted so badly to become marines. Some were near tears. Others would plead their cause to anyone who would listen. We could only hear the questions: Why, why, why? Never the answers. I thought if that happened to me, I would just die. Then it happened.

We lined up for a final inspection. The sergeant and the doctor reviewed our papers. They looked us over, commented, and checked us out one by one. Finally, it came my turn. The sergeant called me over.

They looked at my papers, and then looked at me. The doctor nodded his head at the sergeant. He ordered me, "Step out of line."

Apprehensively standing there, I had to wait until all hands were processed. The doctor and the sergeant approached me. The doctor spoke softly, "How old are you, son?"

"Nineteen years old," I replied quickly.

"Do you have proof, like a birth certificate?" the doctor continued.

"No, sir, I don't, but the Newark recruiting sergeant will vouch for my age. I showed him my birth certificate when I enlisted and I'm sure it has been recorded."

"Son, everything's been recorded, but we want to see it in our hands, view it with our own eyes," the doctor continued sarcastically. "We don't believe you. Either produce your birth certificate or you don't go." I told them I lived in New Jersey. "Sorry," they informed me, "but that's how it is."

I thought for a moment. "How long do I have before they leave?" I asked the sergeant.

"About an hour," he replied. Then to spur me on, he added, "You can make it if you hurry."

"That's twenty-eight miles."

"So what?" he screamed. "We'll hold the bus for fifteen minutes. Get going!"

I know he was aggravated, but I had to ask him one more important question. "Can I use your phone?"

"Go ahead, but hurry it up! It's for government use only!" he hollered.

"Well," I retorted, "this is government business."

He looked at me, exasperated, throwing his hands in the air, and exclaimed, "Go ahead, go ahead! You're giving me a goddamn headache!" He walked away.

I gave the telephone operator my mother's phone number, and my sister Janet answered it on the eighth ring. "Boy, you're lucky. We were just leaving," she said.

"For where?" I inquired.

"New York Penn Station. That's where you're leaving from," she informed me. "We called the recruiting office in Newark, and they told us you would be leaving around noontime."

I could feel that she felt proud of herself for relating such vital information. Janet was like that. She always wanted to be one step ahead of me, a real smarty-cat. It made her feel important and built up her ego. "Listen, sis, I won't be leaving from anywhere if you don't get my birth certificate over here! You see, they don't believe I'm nineteen years old! They won't swear me in until I show them proof of age." I outlined a plan. "Meet me in Penn Station in half an hour. Bring my birth certificate." Kiddingly, I added, "You'll be doing me and your country a great favor! Tell Ma not to worry. If I miss that train today, I'll join the navy tomorrow. We'll have another party."

She ended the conversation by saying, "Oh no, not that. We couldn't live through another one of these enlistments! I'll be there."

"Okay, I will see ya," and I hung up.

Leaving my shoebox (full of goodies) with the recruiting sergeant, I ran out of the office. Down the stairs I ran, taking four steps at one time. Out the building and through the streets of New York I ran. Down the ramp of the Courtland Station I flew. I stopped to get a ticket, and finally, I boarded the train. A few minutes later, we headed for Newark, fourteen miles away.

Connections between New York and Newark were perfect. I ran down the escalator and saw my sister Jan in the distance. I waved and she came toward me. Without saying a word, she handed me the envelope with my birth certificate in it. I kissed her good-bye and, like the anchorman in a relay race receiving the baton, I took off in a burst of speed for the tube train. I was New York bound. Once on that train, I was confident that I would win this race against time.

When I arrived in New York, I had five minutes to reach the recruiting station, running the entire way. I produced my birth certificate to the sergeant. He was smiling now and kiddingly he said, "You certain this is your certificate?" I just glared at him. He got the message. "Okay, okay. Raise your right hand." I was sworn into the corps. I was now a United States Marine.

Everyone was already on the bus when I boarded it with the sergeant. Relatives and friends were saying good-byes to the new recruits. These must have been the relatives from the men from New York, for the seven men who came over with me this morning came alone. As the bus pulled out, I let out a sigh. It was a sigh of relief. I was utterly exhausted.

Our bus headed for New Jersey. The entrance to the Holland Tunnel lay directly ahead. I couldn't help but think of my family heading for New York Penn Station. What a surprise they were in for; what a disappointment, and whoo, would they ever be pissed off! What a tongue-lashing three women were going to give that marine recruiter for giving them false information. Yes, today was going to be one hell of a day for a few people!

I sat alone in front of the bus. With nothing better to do, I started to analyze the faces of the new recruits—twenty-one of us. Everyone was quiet now, even the three smart-asses who seemed to know everything there was to know about the Marine Corps. Without an audience, their boastfulness evaporated. No one slept. All faces bore a somber expression. The eyes told a story. They were looking, but thoughts were far, far away. You could tell they were thinking of home, and our journey hadn't even begun.

We entered Central Station at Jersey City and were quickly herded to a desolate side track to await our train. This was the last place in the world I ever imagined we would leave from. The large iron gates separated us from the other passengers. It wasn't long before our train backed into the depot. We boarded immediately and at 12:45 p.m. pulled out of the station. There was no fanfare, no good-byes. No one cared that we left. Everything was so quiet. Leaving this the station made me realize that things would never be the same. We were riding out, leaving an old life behind. On the horizon, a new life was waiting.

CHAPTER IV

We arrived in Union Station, Washington DC around six o'clock that evening. The station was one mass of confusion. People from all walks of life were trying to make connections. Sergeant Krauser, the recruiter, accompanied us from New York. He had made arrangements for us to have dinner in the station. The restaurant was one of the better ones, and preparing our tables would take at least fifteen to twenty minutes. We preferred to wait outside the fashionable station restaurant. This afforded us an opportunity to view the interior of this large railroad station. From our little corner, we quietly observed the procedure of human elements as well as the station's structural aspects.

At first glance, the interior of Union Station reminded me of a dirigible hanger base; it was so vast and so high. Looking back, the station's interior was dingy and dirty. Billows of smoke hung like large blue clouds from the rafters. Beyond the girders, I saw bursts of sunlight reflecting sunbeams like arrows, pouring and slashing their way down through the skylights. Huge plumes of smoke gave a bluish tint to the clouds. Despite the station's worn-out and shabby appearance, it was far from depressing. On the contrary, seeing this station for the first time, to me, was refreshingly interesting, exciting, even educational.

From my vantage point, I saw hundreds of people scattered in every direction. Folks were milling around in front of the departure gates, while others were congregating in select circles of friends and relatives. It seemed that every nook, cranny, and corner of this building buzzed with action. People were constantly coming or going. The public address system blared away, announcing arrivals and departures of trains in such rapid succession that it was hard to keep track! Your ears grew accustomed to the continual drone of noise. Only the volume changed, depending on the screams of children and the "oohs" and "aahs" of the adults, reacting to the announcements of arrivals and delays. Facial expressions on these people fascinated me—the joys surrounding arrivals, the hellos and good-byes, concerned expressions, embraces, kisses, and handshakes. This wasn't merely emotion, this was life! Feelings were being enacted all around us, not once but repeatedly. Over and over! You became aware of things that you never knew existed. Watching all this unfold made you understand more of life. These were your people. You witnessed the stress of tensions, tears of sorrow, and emotional tears of joy. Different colors of uniforms signified each branch of the armed forces. The redcaps carrying or pushing luggage proved that America was on the move. Truly, this station was the hub. From this point on, your journey took on new meaning, whether you were headed north or south. Washington DC was never considered the heart of the nation, but it was the brains. After this night's observations, though, you couldn't prove it by me.

The sergeant called us to order. The restaurant had prepared our tables. We were hungry as bears. They told us we could have as many dinners as we could eat, provided we didn't change the order. Most of us ordered roast beef, and you could rest assure that Uncle Sam was paying for two dinners for all of us that night.

We boarded the next train at 8:45 p.m. standard time. This train would penetrate the real South—the Deep South, where they still were fighting the Civil War and black people would be told by conductors to sit in the last two coach cars. For me, it was nothing short of culture shock. I had grown up in what you would call a mixed neighborhood. There were immigrants from every place—Irish, Hungarian, Italian, Polish, black, white, pink, and purple! Before this trip, I hadn't even given it a second thought. The older family members and extended relatives tended to keep to themselves, but we kids all played together. We grew up together; that's how cities are. We met at CYO dinners, church picnics, pep rallies, and every other thing you could imagine.

In retrospect, I was lucky. I played ball, every sport you can name. All the boys in the area congregated at the "boys park," and to participate in that was an Olympics in itself. By the time we got to high school, we all fit into a pecking order—a hierarchy of football, baseball, basketball, canoe rowers, swimmers, and skaters. Our lives revolved around ball games. My best buddies were like me, serious about play and good sports. Chums after the play was over, regardless of what team won or lost. It never did matter what your color; it was about how good you could play. I credit the coaches for instilling this practice of good sportsmanship and mutual respect which became so ingrained that it was a habit. Looking back, the coaches eliminated any hostile feelings or grudges. It wasn't permitted.

Now I realized, as the blacks were told "where to sit" on a goddamned train, what a different world it was out there. Half the fellows on the teams I played on were black. I had never given it a second thought before that train ride. The realization was sobering. After my father died, I spent a lot of time being told where to sit (it was a shitty feeling) both figuratively and literally. It was shitty, a shitty way to treat people. It made me a tough, strong, but an angry young man—but mostly strong. At first glance, I felt an understanding and compassion for these people. Deep down, however, I knew that they were stronger than 90 percent of the people I was sitting with.

As they filed to the back cars, I watched their faces. I nodded. A few returned my gaze and nodded back. Mostly they looked down and averted any eye contact. I would soon have a deeper insight to what this ass-backward culture was about. At the time, I didn't know that the only thing a Southerner hated more than the blacks were the Yankees. And I was a real Yankee.

The train itself was an old one. Upon closer observation, we found out that it had gas lights. *They dug deep when they pulled this one out of mothballs!* I thought to myself. It was a real Jesse James special, an "Old Iron Horse."

As we entered the outdated coach car looking for vacant seats, our eyes immediately became aware of the decor from an earlier age— "early American" colonial. Any decorator would have classified it as "early Halloween." The car was painted a ghoulish green, definitely not painted to be attractive to the eye of the passenger, but applied out of dire necessity. The fabric on the high-cushioned seats was green if you examined it carefully, but the seats were so soiled and raggedy-looking, they appeared to be stained black! The windows were dirty, and the windowsills were rotting away. The dimly lit car helped to cover the filthy floor, and fortunately hid yet other areas seriously in need of repair.

The weather was hot, hot and sticky. We opened every window in the car. It helped to empty the foul, musty air which seemed to have been held up in there for ages. When the train started to move, soot from the locomotive's smokestack flew into the open windows, adding to the discomfort of already weary passengers. Soot penetrated our nostrils and blackened them with coal dust. Because of the intense heat, we were sweating profusely. Our clothing stuck to us like glue. My new clothes—well, they looked like hell.

Looking at the wreck we were riding in, it was remarkable that once the train started to move, it didn't break up and fall apart. This train didn't *clickety-clack* over the tracks like most trains. Instead, it squeaked and it squawked. Combined with rocking and rattling, it made the passengers more than a wee bit apprehensive and uneasy. The train was traveling at a slow pace, and as it chugged along in motionless fashion, the engines strained at the bit. But the whistles? They were in fine fettle. They kept blowing, loud and clear, announcing our arrival at every one-horse town. We stopped for everything that was anything, and because of our slow speed, we didn't miss even one tank town.

At every whistle-stop, we took on more and more people. Passengers stood in the aisles, sitting on their suitcases. Others held their belongings wrapped in paper. They stared into space, oblivious to everything and anyone around them. Young women, pretty women with squalling, tired babies, struggled to stand up in the swaying car, peering down on us with squinty, tired eyes. These women followed their husbands to the army camps, some not knowing if they would have any lodging tonight, others not even knowing if their husbands would be there when they arrived. Some of these women had traveled clear across the country to be with their men, traveling in day coaches. They hadn't seen a bed in a week. Determination, hope, and love had carried them this far. They would not be denied. Talk about pioneer spirit; these were pioneers! All of us future marines had gallantly given up our seats to these women, children, and old people. They looked so weary and forlorn. This was definitely not the time to be traveling.

We arrived in North Carolina at midnight. It seemed like we had pulled off the main track over one hundred times to let special trains go by. This had been such a tiresome ride, and God, was it hot! Looking around the dimly lit car, it seemed like 95 percent of the passengers were sleeping and passed out from sheer exhaustion. This was a most uncomfortable car. Theirs was a fitful sleep. All noise had ceased. The whistles weren't blowing and aside from the clickety-clack, it was now quiet and peaceful.

When we reached the Fort Bragg stop, half of the train emptied out. It was amazing how many people the train could accommodate. They stretched in a never-ending line. We finally did get seats, and oh, how good it felt to sit down again and stretch out. It was cooler now, and the night breezes felt invigorating, but I was hungry. In fact, I was starving. I remembered my mother packing me lunch in a shoebox. The box took quite a beating, but the contents were all intact. I opened the lid and feasted my eyes on a whole fried chicken, hard-boiled eggs, corn bread, candy, raisins, and two boxes of cookies. I spread it out on the empty seat before me. It gave the appearance of an Italian picnic. I was enjoying myself immensely, continuing to stuff my face, when two marine recruits came over, just watching me eating away. I looked up at them and asked if they would like a piece of chicken. They didn't refuse, and in no time at all, the rest of the marines were helping themselves to my lunch. Everything disappeared quickly. In the process of eating, we had a few good laughs. The ice was broken. We were getting to know each other, and this was good.

Bill Pierce was from Nutley, New Jersey. He was a former All-State football player. A tall boy with sandy-colored hair and a regular guy with a good sense of humor, we soon became staunch friends. Then there was Forrest E. Corr from West Paterson, New Jersey. His father was a Broadway actor. At this time, he was playing in *Arsenic and Old Lace* and was portraying Col. Teddy Roosevelt. Forrest promised that when we returned to New York City, he would get us free tickets for any evening performance. Forrest Corr was a nice chap, a young Humphrey

Bogart type. He was a domineering person who hated the army with a passion. He tried to force this opinion on his friends, without much success.

There was Joe Setzer. Joe was one of the nicest guys anyone would ever hope to meet. He lived in Woodside, Long Island, and was a big man. He spoke softly and never knocked anyone. He possessed a gentle, polite mannerism that just oozed character and good upbringing. He was a semi-pro baseball player, yet never bragged about any of his achievements. He was a Yankee fan and so was I, so we talked for hours about the old and the new Yankees.

Milo Panos, of Greek descent from lower Manhattan, was another fellow who became my buddy. He was, without a doubt, the hippest guy in the outfit. You could tell that he was from the Big Apple, just by his appearance. He was a sharp dresser, and his speech—he was so well spoken that I couldn't believe a New Yorker didn't have an accent. He was a quiet person too, and really sharp. Being a buyer of men's shoes for Macy's Department Store, Milo knew all the answers. He was a shrewd card player as well as a dice expert. Above all, he was a real ladies' man. He liked me and said that when his sister came to visit our camp, I would be the only one he would trust to go out on a date with her!

And so it went. From small talk to girl talk, to home, the war, and anything that popped into our heads. All night long, we rode in that cattle car, and we talked and talked. Between the clickety-clack, the jerks, the sudden stops, and the pullovers, we didn't get much sleep. In our quest for peace and quiet, we moved from one rattletrap car to another without better results. The musty, stagnant smell of old leather seats gave the speculation and suspicion that some of the passengers weren't sleeping—they were dead.

Despite the inconveniences and the hardships we encountered, everyone we met gave us the same salutation: "Where you young'uns heading for?"

Enthusiastically we answered, "Parris Island."

They would look at us in bewilderment. One distastefully exclaimed, "Parris Island! God, man! You'll be sorry. That place is worse than Devil's Island."

Cutting his conversation off, I sputtered, "Were you ever there?"

He retorted sarcastically, "Hell no, boy! Give me more credit for having more brains than that!" In a Southern drawl, he continued, "I live in these heah parts and I done hear nuff dang stories 'bout that damn place! Good luck!" And he left. And so it went, rumors and more rumors.

For the next few hours we were quiet, alone with our thoughts. We had run out of conversation. I, too, fell into a fitful sleep.

The next thing I knew, the conductors were hollering in all directions. "Yamasee Junction, next stop. Yamasee Junction! Connections for Parris Island! Get your bags! Yam … mmmmmm … a … seeeeeee! All out for Parris Island!" We gathered our equipment and exited the train. It felt strange to have my feet once again on terra firma. It was a long journey, but we made it.

We arrived in Yamasee, South Carolina, around two in the afternoon. The sun was beating down mercilessly on the hard dirt roads of this little town as we trudged along. I could only describe it one way: it was bastardly hot.

Yamasee, South Carolina, was a sleepy little town of approximately three hundred people. As I recall, it was kind of a lazy, hazy place. It had one general store in the center of town. If memory serves me correctly, it was the only building in town, and it stood out predominantly as the proverbial tree that grew in Brooklyn. We didn't see any white people on the streets, only black people. Huddled in small groups along the way, they paid little or no attention to us as we walked past. In fact, you could tell that they more or less accepted this kind of traffic in their town. We were told by authorities to keep together, and in due time, a truck would arrive to take us to the marine base. Parris Island was indeed an island.

We headed for the general store, marching in one large group and commenting on the way about the size of the town and the heat. As we entered the general store, the proprietor met us at the door. He was a black man—not that it made any difference, but I immediately took a mental note, and it stayed with me through the years, that the fact remains that general store owners, blacks or whites, look and act the same. They're the same breed, all business and watching out for pilfering, just like my grandfather. He was a big man and wore a white shirt. With one hand he held the door, and in the other a large cigar. This was 1942, and in the Deep South. When we entered his store, we immediately knew who the boss was, and that he was your equal. He sold everything, and surely had a thriving business with the latest modern conveniences of the day. Large overhead fans looked like airplane propellers, and it was nice and cool in his shop. He was indeed the proud proprietor. Yes, he welcomed us with his quick eye and a slow grin, never laughing, always strictly business. His clerks were all positioned. "Get it now, fellas," he bellowed. "Once on that rock, no soda, candy, or ice cream for boots, and don't forget your money belts." Of course, it was a gimmick to spend more money, or soon we would realize.

For the next two hours we stayed in that store, eating, drinking, and playing the pinball machines. After a while, we grew restless and decided to leave. There were no signs of marines anywhere, coming or going.

Having had our fill of goodies, all of us future marines now headed for the river. It was located on the outskirts of town, and as we neared the water, it was a beautiful sight to behold. Large trees lined the riverbanks and Spanish moss hung down like curtains, its edges skimming the water, creating circles and ripples as it swayed in the soft, summer breeze. In the background, more trees and woods abounded in the area, giving us the impression that we were alone in paradise. We lay down on the soft, velvet mattresses of grass, staring out at the rippling, clear water, reflecting on the beauty surrounding us. God was everywhere.

In the distance, we heard voices and slowly came back to reality. Straining our eyes, we saw a rowboat come into view from a bend in the winding river. Its occupants were young black boys between ten and twelve years of age. They got out of the rowboats and came toward us. They approached and they hollered in loud voices, "Anybody want their oil changed?" Again they repeated the offer, only this time louder: "Anybody want their oil changed?"

"What's that, son?"

A young boy, no more than ten, answered us. "Man, you guys are dumb! Do you want to get laid? Poontang, man, poontang."

We looked at them in utter surprise. They were young pimps. They continued to rave on! "Once you go over to that rock, man, yo ass is going to suck! No poontang there, man. Get it here. Young heads too, man! Get it now!" We stood in shock. They were just wasting their time. There were no takers. They realized it too. Looking at us in disgust and cursing us out, they departed, leaving us once again to our thoughts.

We had now been in Yamasee for five hours with nary a sign of a marine. We were still lying on the grass just relaxing, bored, waiting, thinking, and watching the sun take a downward twist. It was starting to set, and the reflection of its rays on the choppy water threw shimmying, silvery objects of shiny sunbeams into the trees, creating an eerie picture. The South was on standard time, and it would get dark earlier now, but no one seemed to care. There was a time when daylight savings time mattered, but now it was immaterial; nothing seemed to matter anymore.

My mind wandered. I thought of home, my family, and my friends. It was just a day away, but it seemed like an eternity. Glancing down, my eyes fell upon my good pants. They were so wrinkled, they looked like a road map and dirty. I felt like a pig. The whole bunch of us looked like hobos.

My stomach was growling from hunger, yearning for good, hot food. Something like a pot roast dinner is what I had in mind—my Ma's pot roast dinner, with lots of mashed potatoes and hot gravy. *Yeah, I think that would pep me up*, I thought to myself. I could visualize the steam rising from the hot dishes and could even smell the aroma of the food. I was being carried away on a memory.

Suddenly, we heard a disturbance at the end of the road. It was trucks. "They're here! They're here! Over here, this way!" Loud noise of men and trucks woke up this sleepy town. (Loud noise was out of place here. It just didn't belong.) That morning, all the townspeople came down to see us off.

Two dark-green marine six-by-six trucks drove up to the area where we were sitting. A young marine corporal hopped out of the truck and came toward us. We observed him closely with mixed reservations. Now, if there is such a thing as looking like a marine, then this young man looked like a marine. He sure impressed all of us. He was of medium height and had a muscular build. His face was clean shaven, and his suntan reflected the contrast from his salty-khaki uniform. His belt was almost white, and his shoes were highly polished. His shirt was form fitting, showing off "muscular anatomy." He wore a campaign hat. He took everything into consideration, and looked as though he just stepped out of the halls of Montezuma!

"Get into the truck, men, and take all your gear with you!" he ordered. By his drawl, we knew he was from the Deep South. In we went, pulling up the slat seats from the sides of the truck. Once we were seated, the corporal got into the cab. "Is everyone aboard?" he barked.

"Yes, sir," we replied.

"Okay, shove off, mate," he shouted to the driver. As we sped away, the townspeople screamed in a general chorus, "You'll be sorry! You'll beeee sorreeee!" We could still hear their chant two blocks away.

No one said a word. I scanned the men's profiles. All faces bore a somber expression. They were deep in thought, lost in thought. Some reflected on the past, others anticipated the future. I, myself, anticipated the future and scanned the horizon, searching for a hint of what lay ahead.

CHAPTER V

The minute we drove onto the marine base, that old familiar chant, "You'll be sorry," caught our ears again and again as platoons of boots recognized the new arrivals and sounded off whenever we appeared. In our civilian clothes, we looked like prisoners of war. It was 8:30 p.m., and it was dark. The little we did see of the base didn't impress us too much. All over the island, boot platoons were still marching, and the cadence count of the marine drill instructors was new to our ears. They almost sang their commands in low or high melodious voices. Truly, it was fascinating, and the sounds of marching feet and clicking heels, all unison, penetrated the stillness of the night, and it sounded like One Big Giant Step.

The weather was still very hot and sticky as our truck pulled up to an empty barracks. The corporal shouted, "All out," and we proceeded to jump off the truck. "Take your gear with you and leave it in the barracks," shouted the corporal. We proceeded to go up the steps of the wooden barracks. "Don't get comfortable," he informed us. "This isn't your quarters. Just leave your gear and fall outside—that is, if you want anything to eat—and do it on the double." We ran in, dropped our gear, and ran out.

Once outside the barracks, we formed two ranks, and a sergeant who never introduced himself proceeded to march us to a mess hall. The mess hall, located a half a mile away from the barracks, was a large building, and once we arrived there we were instructed by the sergeant, "When you finish eating, come out here, and you stay here. Ya heah me, boy? Stay heah as a group and don't go wandering off. Ya heah me? Stay right heah, even if I don't come back for five hours." He then marched us into the mess hall. The large building seemed to contain hundreds of tables with benches underneath them. Practically all the lights were out except in the front area where we were being seated. We sat at the tables and the mess boys brought out the food, and they served family style. "Delicious menu tonight, fellas," announced the mess boy as he laid down trays of meat at the other end of the table. "Horse cock."

"What did he say?" I inquired to the guy sitting on my left.

"He said horse cock, a terminology of speech used in the corps to describe meat cold cuts."

How vulgar, I thought to myself.

Looking at the meat on the large platter, it wasn't fancy and it wasn't appetizing either. There was Spam, ham, bologna, and liverwich, and it was butchered with a knife, thick as hell and just as inviting. Even the bread was cut on a bias, with one end two inches thick and piled on the table in such disorder and length that it looked like a small replica of the Rocky Mountain range. And the pickles looked like a school of sharks swimming in a barrel. The only thing that looked inviting were the pitchers of milk located on both ends of the table. The mess boy stated that if we wanted any seconds to just holler "Survey" and that they would refill the dish. Our faces reflected our distaste for the menu, and the mess men sensed it. Occasionally, they would blurt out, "Come on, gentlemen, you're not eating. Don't let all this food go to waste."

I tried to get two pieces of bread to meet. It was impossible. I was hungry, but the ham, such as it was, was the only thing that appealed to me. I trimmed it into small pieces and cut off the thick skin, and I made a sandwich—one was enough for me. But I did drink a pitcher of milk.

Once finished eating, we gathered outside in a group and waited for the sergeant to reappear (no one left the area).

In the next hour, we accomplished two hours of work. The sergeant took us to the supply depot, where we drew a mattress, a mattress cover, a pillow, two sheets, a pillowcase, and two woolen blankets. Then we marched in the sand to our barracks, located about two and a half miles from this area. We were a motley-looking crew as we marched along trying to hold our bulky equipment. It kept sliding, slipping, and falling to the ground. We kept picking it up and somehow we arrived at our destination with our equipment intact. We were tired and sweaty. The weather was hot and sticky as we approached the wooden structure that would be home for the next three months. There wasn't a breeze blowing as we entered the building with our cumbersome load, but we did have guests. There were at least forty boots already there.

The sergeant disappeared once we arrived, and a Corporal Howard took over our outfit. He was a nice-looking man in his early twenties who looked every inch a marine. He had short blond hair, blue eyes, and was deeply tanned. His posture was very straight, almost rigid. He introduced himself as Cpl. Robert E. Howard from Mobile, Alabama, who would be our assistant drill instructor, henceforth called DI for short. He was dressed in a starched khaki uniform, and his shirt was open at the collar, and he was wearing a starched khaki overseas cap, commonly called a piss cutter by the marines.

Corporal Howard then schooled us in how to make a military bed. We were told to observe closely, as he neatly folded the hospital corners and then proceeded to create a margin of about eight to ten inches from the head of the bed, folding the blanket and the sheet together, then tucking the blanket all around it, giving the appearance of a tight, smooth sack. He then made up another bunk and stressed the point that the sergeant wouldn't tolerate a bed that was not made up right.

We were all assigned bunks, and I took notice that they were all made of iron. They were two bunks high, one on top of each other. I wanted a top bunk and Milo Panos wanted a bottom one, so we shared one together. Next to us were Forrest Corr on the bottom and Bill Pierce on the top. On our other side were Harry Pinto on the bottom and Joe Setzer on the top. We then helped each other make up our bunks.

Corporal Howard then proceeded to explain and define the terminology used in referring to the barracks that we were living in. He started off, "The Marine Corps is a branch of the navy, and navy terminology is used wherever it can be applied. The doors become ports, the stairs become ladders, the walls become bulkheads, and the floor becomes the deck. The room is divided into two parts, fore and aft. The sides are thus divided into port side and starboard side. To your left is the port, to your right is the starboard side. Leaving the base is called going ashore, and when you have leave it is called liberty. Liberty is divided into two parts, called watches: the starboard watch and the

portside watch. Only half of the personnel can go ashore at one time …,"
and so on and on it went.

After we had squared our gear away, Corporal Howard informed
us to stand by our bunks and that the sergeant in charge of our platoon
would be out to inspect us. He went on to tell us a little about the
sergeant. He was a veteran of ten years' service in the USMC. Had seen
China service, was involved in the Pinay incident, was the best boxer
in the Marine Corps in the light heavyweight division. Didn't have one
mark against his record and was a stickler for discipline, orderliness, and
self-control. His name was Sgt. Robert E. Horton and he hailed from
Beaufort, Georgia. I realized then that quite a few of these Southerners
were named after Robert E. Lee, the Confederate general, but I never
dreamed I would meet so many of them in one day. Corporal Howard
then dismissed us but said to stay in the area. It was a busy day, and I
had a feeling it was going to be a busy night.

Then as I was packing away some clothes, I thought I heard my name
called. I cocked my ear, listening intently above the noise and chatter
of sixty-five men. Then again I heard it. "Pvt. Hank Summers, report
immediately to Sergeant Horton's office." There was no mistaking it now.
What did he want with me?

I went directly to his office. The door was partly open. I knocked
once and peeked in. Sitting at the desk was Sergeant Horton. He looked
up at me with a scowl and before he could say one word, I blurted out,
"Did you call me, sir?" That was it. What transpired in the next fifteen
minutes was the most shocking eye-opener imaginable.

With a snarled expression, Sergeant Horton screeched, "Whar yu
frum, boy?"

"New Jersey, sir," I replied.

Reflecting for a few seconds, "Ah thot so! Only a goddamn dumb
Northerner could act like you, boy."

My faced flushed and my blood boiled. "What did I do wrong, sir?"
I coolly asked him.

"Shut yo goddamn mouth, boy. I ask the questions heah. Get me,
boy? Get me! Ah ask the questions heah!"

I stood in silence, dumbfounded. I really didn't know what to do. He scanned me from head to toe, and then stood up and proceeded to walk around me like a panther stalking his prey—getting ready to pounce. I observed him nervously, pretending to ignore his glaring eyes. In his hand was a swagger stick, and he kept tapping it on his trousers as he marched around me. He had a ruddy complexion and although his face was expressionless, it was flushing red. His hair was sandy, and he had squinting green eyes. He had a good build and the collar on his shirt was open, thus exposing a bull-like neck. When he spoke, his jugular veins stood out like two drainpipes on a house. Any minute now I was expecting that whip across my face, but it never happened.

Then as if he was reading my mind, he spoke in a low drawl. "Never anticipate the command, boy!" And in a still louder voice he repeated, "Don't you ever anticipate the command." Looking directly in my eyes, he continued, "You know what that means, boy? Don't ever react before the order or command is given. And now you go out there and stand at attention at the foot of your bunk. I'm not finished with you yet." He then dismissed me, and I walked out of his office.

My face surely must been flushed as I walked to my bunk. I was burning underneath, for I felt that some Southern SOB had surely kicked me square right in the ass. Walking directly to my bunk, I had twenty new boots moving right along with me and curiously asking all sorts of questions like: Did he hit you? What did you do? Did he hurt you? What happened? I didn't even get to my bunk or get the opportunity to say one word before I heard the command, "Atten … shion" in a loud, clear voice.

The voice bellowed again, "Atten … shion!" I turned around and Sergeant Horton, with his hands on his hips, was standing in the middle of the barracks. His face was red with anger as he blurted out almost in a snort, "Freeze! Goddamn you, boy, freeze! That's it, that's it, like statues. Don't move, boy!" It was now quiet, very quiet.

Then Sergeant Horton started to roar. "Now listen to this. Whenever I come out that door, no matter when, the nearest boot will yell, 'Atten … shion.' Then, you'll stand so rigid that you will think they stuck a broomstick up your ass. Furthermore, I don't even want to see your ears wiggle. Get me? Okay! Now, at ease. We're going to do this over once more, and we're going to do it right. You, boy!" pointing to Harry Pinto. "When I come out that door, I want you to yell, 'Atten … shion!' " He continued to rave, "When you holler, boy, I want to see that roof raise one foot. And if you don't," he snarled, "yo Yankee ass is going to suck buttermilk." With that last remark, he disappeared into his office and closed the door.

Five, ten, fifteen minutes crawled by. Everything was quiet. In all that time, I don't think anyone moved one foot in either direction. Despite ourselves, we were all anticipating his entrance. Every one of us had one eye glued to the office door, waiting, waiting, just waiting for God Almighty to walk out.

It never happened that way. Before anyone realized it, Sergeant Horton had come in the front door, and he was almost in the middle of the room before half a dozen boots recognized him simultaneously and blurted out "Atten … shion!" in such a manner that it sounded as if they were spitting out their teeth.

Sergeant Horton was furious, absolutely raving. Cursing, swearing continuously, he commanded us to line up in front of our bunks. Then his order came. He roared, "Attenn … shion!" and by God, the roof did lift two feet. At least it seemed to, and for sure we boots jumped two feet. But Sergeant Horton wasn't satisfied. His voiced boomed, "There are sixty-two of you shitheads here. Now I don't want to hear sixty-two assholes clicking all over this place. I want to hear one click, all in unison. Ya heah me, boy! One big asshole, one big click. Now we're going to do it again." And he screamed, "Att … tenn … shion. Again. Att … tenn … shion. Again. Att … tenn … shion. God damn, you bunch of shitheads. You're going to do it in unison or we're going to be here all night. Now do it again. Ten … shion. Again. Att … ten … shion."

Around the hundredth time, it started to resemble one big click. We knew that he wasn't satisfied, but he had other things on his mind—and did he ever have things on his mind. First he put us at attention, and he kept us at that position. Then he proceeded to go to the middle of the squad room. Deliberately, taking his sweet-ass time, he marched up and down the room, swinging his swagger stick, observing his new men, looking each one over one by one, trying to analyze each and every one of us.

Then like a lion eyeing his prey, he made directly for his victim, and it was Milo Panos. The sergeant didn't waste any time. "Where you from, boy?" he screamed.

"New York City, sir," Panos replied.

"That's the asshole state of the Union, boy! You know that, don't you?" No answer. "Don't you?" Still no answer. "You know that, shitbird! Don't you?" his voice boomed.

"Yes, sir," replied Panos.

"Then tell everyone, and say it loud," the sergeant commanded.

"New York is the asshole of the Union," Panos hollered in a loud voice.

"Say it again, shitbird, and louder," retorted Sergeant Horton.

Panos screamed, "New York is the asshole state of the Union."

Now the boots began to snicker and giggle. This infuriated the sergeant. He immediately grabbed four new recruits and ordered them to do twenty-five push-ups. Three of them couldn't make it, and he proceeded to humiliate them and berated them unmercifully. He also threatened to have them court-martialed, and he promised the next son of a bitch who laughed would stand at attention for the next twelve hours. The silence in that room was deafening.

Again, the sergeant approached a recruit from Lynn, Massachusetts. His name was Joe Dowd. Joe was a tall, lanky lad with a Bostonian accent. Sergeant Horton sized him up from head to toe, and you could almost feel his beady eyes going through the body of the young boot. His piercing voice rang out, splitting the silence. "Where ya from, boy?"

"Lynn, Massachusetts, sir."

The sergeant's eyes lit up like neon signs. "Well! Lookee heah," announced the sergeant in a surprised manner. "A real Yankee Doodle. Yes sir, a real Beantown boy. A genuine all-Yankee shithead, and I can tell you don't know shit from shinola." Then sizing him up once again, he continued, "How old are you, boy?"

"Nineteen, sir," was the reply.

"Well, you better keep your nose clean, boy! 'Cause we love you real Yankees down heah."

With that remark, he proceeded to the next recruit and so on down the line, until he interviewed each one of us. It was after 11:00 p.m. now but time meant nothing to Sergeant Horton. He strode up and down the squad room floor, looking, always looking, just daring one of us to make a move, hoping that we would, but all of us were still standing at attention.

He then proceeded to give us an orientation speech. With his swagger stick still in his right hand always smacking against his pants leg, he continued to pace the floor from one end of the barracks to the other. His booming voice signified that he would only speak once it was quiet—real quiet. Then he began.

"Yours is not to reason why, but to either do or die." Then letting us digest that statement, he continued, "All of you men are beginning a new life here in Parris Island. All of you are Yankees, and we might as well begin there. Forget you ever were a Yankee. Forget you ever were a civilian. Forget your parents, your sweethearts, your dear ones, forget you ever had a home." Then stressing a point, "This is your home now, and this is where your life begins. During the next few months, we will try to make a marine out of you. And looking at this sad-ass group, very few of you will make it. But the ones that do, you'll be good marines, and you'll belong to the best damn fighting outfit in the world—the United States Marines. Our mutual enemy is one tough son of a bitch. He is a dedicated soldier who is willing to give his life gladly for his country, for his emperor, and his Rising Sun flag. He will stop at nothing to achieve his goal, but a well-trained marine is worth seven goddamn Japs. Yes, seven rotten, freaking Nips, and don't you ever forget it. Parris Island is the factory where we build marines. This is the product stamped 'Made in America.'

"There are a few other things I want you to remember, and boy, you better never forget. The Marine Corps owns your ass, body and soul. They can work you twenty-four hours a day. I'm your god, and I give the commands. I say do and you do. I say shit and you'll shit. There will be no pogey-bait marines in my outfit. That means no candy, ice cream, or cake all the while you're here. All your packages will be inspected by Sergeant Horton—that's me. Then if you wish to speak to me, you will always speak in the third person. As an example: Private Jones wishes to speak to Sergeant Horton. This is a very important subject with me, so don't you ever forget it. Also, don't ever anticipate the command. This can be applied to your whole life, so keep that in mind. If you're on a company street, remember to salute all officers and all officer vehicles. Yes, even if their wives are driving the car. Your right hand is going to be up more than down. Failure to comply to this order can result in disciplinary action or a court-martial. Incidentally, all officers' license plates are yellow, so you will have no difficulty identifying them.

"One more thing: never talk back to a noncommissioned officer, even if you are right. Remember, this is a capital sin in the Marine Corps and will never be tolerated. If you do, we will make one hell of an example of you—we will beat your goddamn brains out, boy—then you will be court-martialed for insubordination and drummed out of the Marine Corps with a dishonorable discharge.

"Now, if you have any bitches, keep them to yourself. Learn to keep your nose clean, and if you're a smart-ass and you think that you know how the corps operates, forget it. As of now, you don't know shit from shinola." He then paused for a minute, but he wasn't through yet.

"I hope you have been listening," he continued. "I try never to repeat myself. If you break any rules or regulations, that's tough shit. I have one side: rotten. I have a job to do, and you can bet your ass I'm going to do it. In the corps, they have a saying that you don't have to do anything that you don't want to. But boy! If you don't, you surer than hell had wished that you had.

"That's all I have to say tonight. Personal hygiene is a must in this camp; therefore, every evening you had better take a shower. Failure to do so, then we will give you one with a wire brush. I'll just say this about shaving: shave whether you need to or not. That's an order. Reveille is at 0500, and you had better hit the deck when those lights go on. Corporal Howard, take over." And with that remark, Sergeant Horton slowly strolled away without turning his head and disappeared into his office.

Corporal Howard dismissed us. My body was numb from standing at attention for the last two hours. No one said a word and then a loud voice hollered, "Lights out in fifteen minutes." In quietness we did our necessary chores. Thoughts were tumbling around in my head like dominoes. I made my way to my sack and finally, I was in between the sheets. The mattress was hard, but at this point that was the least of my worries, and I didn't give a damn. I was so tired, so exhausted, so weary—yes, so everything. Today if you had a day like this, you would be in a state of depression, but in 1942, you were just shocked. At least that's the way it affected me. I couldn't believe it. I just couldn't believe that I had volunteered to fight for my country, and to die if necessary for it, and that my country could be so ungrateful as to treat me as a common criminal.

I tried to put these thoughts out of my head, but they kept returning over and over again. I couldn't fall asleep. I was so keyed up at this point that nothing seemed right. I had to think things out now. I was utterly and thoroughly disgusted and confused, besides being disillusioned. Imagine these goddamn Southerners. We're in a world war, and they're still fighting the Civil War. I knew one thing: I hated all Southerners. I hated their goddamn guts, and this Sergeant Horton, I already hated this SOB with a passion. I hated him so much that I already was thinking that he should die, but any kind of death would be too good for this Southern SOB.

Thus, with hate on my mind and murder in my heart, I turned over on my stomach and looked out the open window. There were no screens, just a window cut out in the side of the building to let in some air, and mosquitoes. They were like dive bombers buzzing around my head. I covered my head with the sheets, leaving only my eyes exposed, and peered out into the dark, still night. In the distance, I could see the moon. It was shining big and bright. Again, I thought, just staring, reflecting; despite the miserable life ahead of me, I could still appreciate God's beauty. It was everywhere. The moonlight flooding the surrounding area made the coarse sand appear like soft snow. It silhouetted the trees, making them appear shrouded against the dark sky, and when the soft winds moved the leaves, they resembled balls of ermine. The stars hung like a coachman's lanterns from the sky and their lights twinkled like sparklers, creating a fairy-land atmosphere.

With these pleasant thoughts in mind, I became drowsy and slowly dozed off into the land of dreams. It was an exhausting, expiring twenty-four hours.

CHAPTER VI

Working days began early in the Marine Corps, but at Parris Island they began especially early. The sound of that brass bugle blasting out "Reveille" at five o'clock in the morning, the turning on of the lights and that dreaded voice screaming, "Hit the deck" were enough to scare the hell out of you. To most of us, five o'clock in the morning was considered the middle of the night. However, like all necessary evils, you gradually grew accustomed to it, and for those who didn't, the corps had ways and means of making you accept it. Panos and myself were on the floor in jig time as were 95 percent of the recruits, but there are always a few dissenters who had to be shown—and shown they were. The sergeant and the corporal walked up those aisles, ripping blankets right off the bunk and pushing the occupants onto the floor, not caring whether they were on the top bunk or the bottom. They threw pails of water right on the bunk, sometimes both drenching the occupants and all their personal belongings. And if that didn't do it, they would knock over the bunk with the sleeping occupants in it. In no time at all, we had 100 percent believers.

As soon as that horn blew, you knew the pace would quicken with each ticking little moment. "Roll call in five minutes," barked the sergeant, and he would continue screaming on down the line. "Fall out for roll call, five minutes." I just had time to get my shoes and pants on when the order came to "Fall out" and you could hear Sergeant Horton screech, "On the double, goddamn it, on the double." Just the sound of that voice, that blasting, booming voice would make your pace quicken, and we ran out of that barracks like chickens flying out of a coop. The company street was black. There were no lights and mass confusion seemed to be taking place, but not for long. That booming voice screamed, "Fall into two ranks and cover down. Forty inches back to breast," then, "Att ... tenn ... shion." We snapped into a rigid position.

Corporal Howard, carrying a flashlight, called the roll. You responded to your last name in a loud, sharp voice, "Here, sir," acknowledging your presence to God Almighty.

Roll call accomplished, Sergeant Horton again took over the platoon. While standing on the barracks steps and looking every inch the bastard that he was, the sergeant proceeded to outline the platoon's procedure for the day. "When I dismiss you now," he stated, "I want you to wash up and shave and then make up your sacks." Again he stressed, "They better be made up right, no sloppy job, square the corners." He went on to tell us to "sweep the decks, then mop the decks, tidy up your gear, and fall out for chow at 0600. After chow, again tidy up the barracks for inspection, and then be prepared to fall out at 0700. Today we will get a clothing issue and a part of our web gear. We will also get a GI haircut." Then as if he remembered something, he stopped short and turned the platoon over to Corporal Howard, who dismissed us to carry out our chores.

At 0600, Corporal Howard marched us to chow. We entered the mess hall as a group. One platoon after another would line up at the tables, and we would stand at attention with our arms folded in front of our mess table. When the last person to enter fell in formation, then the NCO Officer of the Day would call out in a loud, clear voice, "Seats," and all the boots would sit down, the food would be brought out by mess-men, and we would be served family style. The breakfast menu on our first morning at Parris Island consisted of creamed chipped beef on toast, which they fondly called "shit on shingle," and which in turn clearly defined it. Just looking at it made me sick. My friend Panos the Greek went back for seconds. I asked him how he could eat that stuff. He replied, "Just close your eyes and pretend it's a French delicacy." Besides that bill of fare on the menu, there were always plenty of other things to eat. They always had stewed figs, prunes, and plums on the menu, in addition to fresh fruit and all the cereal you could eat, plus all the milk you could drink. Toast, marmalade, jellies, and peanut butter by the gallon. When it came to chow, there was always plenty to eat, and that was one thing we couldn't complain about. Furthermore, when your stomach was full, they could work you more. Summing it up, we couldn't brag that this was a plain and fancy restaurant, because it wasn't. It was just portrayed as food, nothing else. But it was in abundance.

Corporal Howard marched us back to our barracks and at 0700, our day began. For the next five hours, we marched all over the area. We marched from one depot to another, collecting gear and supplies. The first item issued was a canvas bag about forty inches high with a hasp attached to the top of it for locking purposes when there were contents in it. This carrier was called a "sea bag." Henceforth, that sea bag would travel anywhere and everywhere that you did. Occasionally it got misplaced, but eventually it turned up somewhere. I never remember one being lost. We stuffed everything into this bag and today, our first stuffing day, it got in its first workout. The original clothing allowance for a marine consisted of the following:

(1) 4 skivvy drawers (white)
(2) 4 T-shirts (white)
(3) 2 sets of dungarees (trousers and jacket)
      2 dungaree caps
(4) 4 khaki shirts
      4 khaki pants
(5) 1 helmet (sun) (pith)
(6) 1 dress blouse (green)
      1 overcoat (green)
      2 trousers (green)
      1 overseas cap (green)
      1 overseas cap (khaki)
      1 pair leather gloves
(7) 1 pair field shoes
      1 pair dress shoes
      4 pair work socks
      2 pair dress socks
(8) 2 belts (khaki)
      2 buckles
      2 scarves (ties)
      Plus ornaments for all uniforms
      1 stamp pad with your name on it for marking your lot set

At the next supply house, we received leggings (canvas), cartridge belt, canteen cover, canteen, first aid pack with cover, a helmet liner, a steel helmet, and mosquito net, plus haversack knapsack, belts, shovel, shovel cover, pick, cooking gear, eating gear, utensils, pole pegs, rope tent, poncho, etc. From the armory, we drew our rifles and bayonets, and they were covered with a grease (protective) from World War I.

Once we had drawn our equipment, we formed two ranks and the sergeant marched us to the Post Exchange. The Post Exchange was located in the main area, the civilized area of Parris Island. We were about four miles from our boondocks home. The main area had red brick buildings and lush green lawns. All the higher-ranked officers lived in this area, and in the distance you could see the commanding officer's mansion. He lived as well or better than any Southern plantation owner, and his slaves were all white.

We had come to the Post Exchange to get our GI haircuts. They had eight civilian barbers working in this exchange, and I don't think one ever graduated from barber school. They had a knack for butchering a head in a matter of minutes. Until you go with sixty-five people for a GI haircut, then you haven't lived. Since our arrival in Parris Island, the men had been so tense and so uptight that in the last twenty-four hours, I hadn't seen one smile or heard one mote of laughter.

We entered the barber shop in relays of eight. As eight men came out, then eight more would go in. The letter in your last name determined who went in first. Everything proceeded in accordance with the letters in the alphabet. It's funny, but men, especially young men, no matter how burly, manly, or rough they may be, are just as conceited or as vain as any woman when it comes to their hair. Hair has always been a touchy, private, sacred subject. Even in the forties, when men wore their hair short, they were still particular about the length and the part. The majority of the men did not want their hair too short—they wanted something to comb—but a butcher GI barber was sadistic in his work. He didn't leave you anything to comb and nothing to grab.

The first eight men who entered this ghoulish chamber got the biggest shock of all. I recall how all the recruits lined up at the windows and watched with anticipation as the men sat in the barber chairs. All faces were serious as the barbers draped the sheets around the boots' necks. The barbers appeared eager to get to work. The sound of the electric head clippers in the barber's hand penetrated through the glass windowpanes, and you knew the job was about to start. We were observing every move he made. He machined up the front, and then down the back and across the sides in neat little furrowed rows. The marine in the chair kept bobbing his head as if trying to steer it away from the machine. All heads were reacting in the same manner. Round and round they went as tons and tons of hair hit the floor. The expression on their faces was one of pain and anxiety combined with fear and disbelief. From their distorted features, I know that they couldn't believe that this thing was happening—it would have been easier to face a firing squad.

When every blade of hair had been weeded from his head and when the mower had mowed every last strand, then the barber removed the towel. The barber said, "Next." The body in the chair didn't move; he heard nothing at all. He kept staring, staring at all that hair on the floor. The barber nudged him to get up. The sad face raised his eyes. The marine who had just been scalped stood up. Again he didn't move; he was in a state of shock, bewildered. He just kept rubbing his bald head, not knowing whether to shit or go blind.

Then the fun began. The oncoming marine, startled, took a gulping, gaping look at the dehaired marine and exclaimed in a high-pitched voice, "Holy Christ!" and sat down in the chair. The bald marine looked down at him. He nervously giggled, and then a short burst of laughter erupted. He tried to hide it with his hand. The bald marine was still looking at him, staring. The one in the chair could control himself no longer. He roared out with laughter. His body shook in a convulsive manner. It started a chain reaction; everyone was laughing. Slowly and quietly, the marines came out of the barber shop and faced their tormentors, and they were greeted with remarks of all kinds. "Good God, look at the knobs on this guy's head." Every head looked different; some were square, some were round. Some had their ears sticking out like wings, some people looked like they could fly. Others had pointed heads, some had flat heads. The first thing you know, everyone was laughing so heartily that it was like a visit to the fun house. Even our sergeant laughed, and that took a lot of doing. Like I said before, you haven't lived until you visit a barber shop with sixty-five marine boots.

Once back in our barracks, we were told to put on our dungarees and our boondockers. The smell of new clothes always has a distinct aroma, and it kinda lifted your spirits. When we were dressed, the sergeant told us to fall out in the company street. Once there, he proceeded to line us up according to height. The tallest man led off, and it gradually tapered down to the shortest, who were called "feather merchants." This formation was to be our permanent formation for as long as our stay on the island.

Sergeant Horton snapped us to attention, and then he addressed us in his usual manner. "This is your permanent formation. When I give the order to fall out, I want to see you fall in formation in a matter of seconds, not minutes. When you organize, you have to start somewhere, and today we started. You all have the same haircut, you wear the same clothes, you'll eat the same food, and as time goes on you'll all look alike and think alike. Tomorrow will be your first full day of training. Put your heart and soul into it, and you'll find it rewarding in the end. Remember, you're all volunteers. That's a plus in your favor. You're all handpicked. Not everyone can be a marine. Physically, you're the cream of the crop, and you have the capabilities of becoming the best fighting men in the world. This is the factory where we build marines. We play no favorites, and we're out to bust your ass; and believe me, we will. This is the place where we find out if you have any guts." Then, scanning all our faces in long, sweeping glances, he turned the platoon over to Corporal Howard, who marched us off to chow.

The time was 1600 navy time (8:00 p.m.. I had taken a shower and a shave and was busy squaring away my gear when Corporal Howard approached me. "Report to Sergeant Horton's office immediately, Private," he informed me.

I took off on the double and knocked on his door. "Come in," he said. Entering the lion's den, I stood at attention in front of his desk and at the same time requested permission to speak with Sergeant Horton. "Permission granted," he replied in a gruff voice.

"Pvt. Hank Summers was asked to report to Sergeant Horton, sir. Could Sergeant Horton inform Private Summers as to what it is, sir?"

He looked at me for a full minute, and then told me to stand at ease. Casually, he told me that I had a visitor outside the barracks. I asked permission in the third person to be dismissed, and he granted me permission, at the same time telling me to leave by the back door.

As I walked out the back door of the wooden barracks, I saw the outline of two shadowy figures. They were standing in the darkness, and as I skipped down the stairs they hurriedly came toward me, almost running. Then, straining my eyes in the blackness, I recognized two old familiar friends. Jack Mulligan and Jimmy Beaumont were grinning from ear to ear. My joy was inconceivable. Abounding with delight, I grabbed one by the hand and the other by the arm. They in turn grabbed my shoulders with their free hand. It was like playing "ring around the rosy." We were jumping with glee. I followed their eyes, and I could see that I was more than a friend—I was a symbolic representation of home, and the first words out of their mouths confirmed it. "How is everything at home?" they said simultaneously. Then we all started to ask questions at the same time. Then we all stopped, looked at each other, and laughed. It was a happy laugh. I motioned to Mull to speak first.

Jokingly, he said, "What the hell are you doing here?"

"Same thing you are," I replied.

"I thought you had more brains," Jim chimed in.

Then, looking behind me to make sure that he wasn't there, I asked them point-blank about Sergeant Horton. "Well, we know one thing. He's an SOB. We were here last night, and he had a bug up his ass and he wouldn't let us see you. But all these Southern sergeants are the same. They're miserable bastards."

I told them how he berated me last night. They said it was par for the course. "All these Southern bastards hate the Northerners." Then I told them, "If I ever see this guy off the base, I'm going to kill him. God! How I hate his goddamn guts, and I've only been here one day."

They advised me to simmer down and try to ignore him. "Take one day at time. Do what he asks you to do, and above all keep your nose clean." They continued, "Time will pass and in no time at all, you'll be leaving on a ten-day furlough. All boots get a ten-day pass when their training is over." They then informed me that their training was over as of today, and they were going home tomorrow. They would give everyone my best regards.

I envied them, but I tried not to let my true feelings show. I told them that they looked terrific, and they sure did. Most of their hair had grown in, but they made fun of me. Mull said I looked like a taxicab coming down the street with its doors open. I questioned them about the training. They said it was rough and hot as hell. The sun hit 120 degrees every day, and no one went through without passing out a few times. Jimmy said Mull passed out at least five or six times, and Mull said Beaumont had two left feet and got all the shit details, besides passing out at least five times himself. I told them to knock it off, and we changed the subject.

After their furlough, they were going to school in Quantico, Virginia. Quantico was thirty-three miles from Washington DC, the best liberty town in the United States. Beaumont had all the statistics. This Washington DC had forty-five women to every one man. Can you imagine what a liberty town that place was? And reflecting, I could hardly wait. "Just get finished up here, Hank, and get yourself stationed up here with us. We will be in school for twelve weeks and what a ball we'll have. Keep that in mind and this boot camp will pass in no time at all."

The conversation finally drifted to home, loved ones, girlfriends, guys who were left and who had gone. Small talk, nice talk. We planned leaves together and the places in New York that we would take our dates. Then we reminisced about our school days, teachers, sporting events, New Year's parties. The year I carried Mull home over my shoulder after he passed out. I walked two miles with him that night, and it was bitter cold. His mother met me at the door, and I marched him into his room and threw him on the bed and walked out. Yes, they were some days.

Then Corporal Howard stepped out and said I had five more minutes to wrap it up. It's funny when you're enjoying yourself, the time always passes by too quickly. We shook hands and just by the squeeze, you knew they were wishing me the best of everything. They promised to drop by and see my family and we would keep in touch. "Good-bye and good luck" were the final words. Then I watched them disappear into the black night.

As I climbed the barracks stairs, I felt quite alone. I turned my head to take one last look in the direction that they disappeared. It was just blackness. I reflected on their presence for a moment. Deep down, I knew a part of me was going home with them.

I entered the barracks. It was very quiet. The bugler was sounding *tat-too*—fifteen minutes to lights out. Another day had come and gone. Another day closer to home.

When the lights did go out, I was in my sack and listening to the bugler playing "Taps." The playing of "Taps" brings all sorts of things to mind. With each musical note, your mind wanders: a soft night, a flood of moonbeams, a gentle breeze, a silhouette. Yes, a lonely silhouette of a man blowing a horn. Sometimes a lonely call in the still of the night like a farewell, a good-bye, a "till we meet again." It's sweet like a gentle kiss, a soft touch, a smattering, a long-lasting look, a cry, a teardrop, a gentleness. Yes! Everything comes to mind—a drifting of memories on soft pillowed clouds, a sweet remembrance of long ago. Someone's calling you; it's in a distance, but you hear it, you feel it. It's a God-keep-you-safe thing, an aesthetic happening, and from afar, a pleasant adieu, bonsoir, sweet dreams.

CHAPTER VII

The first day of basic training began at 0700 navy time. When the order came to fall out, we lined up in company formation according to height. The uniform of the day was dungarees and pith helmet. The cartridge belt was worn with a canteen of water. Sergeant Horton instructed us that the first few days we would get infantry drill and individual instructions without arms (weapons). Everything was done by the numbers, and it was amazing how fast we progressed. There seemed to be a thousand commands, from saluting to steps in marching, from quick time to double time, from rear marching to facing front, back step, side step, half step, change step, from flank marching to column marching, and from eyes right or left to rests and halts. For three hours straight, we did nothing but learn commands. Sergeant Horton did nothing but screech and scream, and he kept you on your toes continually. I had to admit he was an excellent teacher. He just didn't impart knowledge; he knocked it into your head physically at times. He was very much in command at all times, and he stressed repeatedly there are two kinds of commands used in close-order drill. They are the preparatory command and the command of execution. Furthermore, he wanted to see smartness and precision in the execution of commands of every detail in drill. He wanted 110 percent, and he got it from his platoons.

The new uniforms were creating a problem, because of the stiffness of the material. It cut into your thighs and calves as you walked, and your elbows and armpits as you swung your arms while walking. The heavier a man was, the more chafing it created. The new shoes were also a problem. They were stiff and blisters developed on your heels as well as your toes. Sergeant Horton was well aware that this was going to happen. It was another one of his cute little games. When someone complained, he would laugh and say, "Tough shit."

Everything in the Marine Corps was "Now," and Sergeant Horton didn't waste any time introducing his new platoon to the boondocks. As soon as we learned a few commands, we were on our way. Now when you arrive in the boondocks, you don't need anyone to describe it for you. Just two lines from a poem called "Parris Island" vividly describes it:

"This is Parris Island, the land that God forgot,

Where the sand is fourteen inches deep, and the sun is scorching hot."

They say that walking and running in sand is one of the best conditioners for your legs, and again Sergeant Horton wasted no time. He tried to get us in condition in one day. We marched and we ran, and we ran and we marched. For five straight hours, we continued this physical exercise, and nary a man dropped out. I think he was amazed at the stamina of this platoon, or perhaps he was hungry, for he marched us in for noonday chow. We were perspiring like horses, and our dungarees were soaking wet. The hot mess hall only made us sweat more, but it was cool by comparison to what was in store for us in the afternoon.

We were back out in the boondocks by one o'clock in the afternoon. The scorching hot sun was unbearable in the afternoons; the temperature would often exceed 120 degrees. But Sergeant Horton seemed to enjoy his work more during these hot hours of the day. He looked cool in his form-fitting salty-khaki uniform. With his pith helmet squared away on his head, he jauntily marched us along, rhythmically singing his cadence in a loud, clear voice, almost with a reverence like a priest on the altar singing a Gregorian chant during a High Mass. It would echo through the air: "A wan ... a reap ... a two ... four ... your leph ... two ... reap ... four ... your leph ... your loaf ... high ... loaf ... your left high loaf." Then in a higher note, "Your right flank ... harsh ... your left flank ... harsh ... to the rear ... harsh ... rip harsh ... rip harsh ... platoon halt ... one ... two."

Then he would start his berating and bark in all directions. "I never saw such a bunch of shitbirds in my whole life. Moore, Jones, you two assholes don't know your left from your right. Panos, where ya from, boy?"

"New York, sir."

"Ah thought so. The asshole of the nation. Boy! You got two goddamn left feet. Novak, just because you're a Polack boy, you don't have to act like one. Snap out of your shit, boy! Now we're going to start again, and I'm not going to stop till your asses are going to be lying in that sand."

He proceeded to march us to an area that had a few trees. It looked like an oasis in the Sahara Desert. Corporal Howard and Sergeant Horton stood under those trees. It looked cool. And then he started to march us up and down those mounds of sand. It was hot and it got hotter. The pace quickened as did the tempo. The heat was unbearable, as the sun reflected from the sand into your eyes. As we double-timed up and down the sand, Sergeant Horton's voice was becoming as unbearable as the heat. Sweat was pouring down our faces, and it was rolling into our eyes like salty, soapy water, creating a burning sensation and blurring your vision. It was most difficult to see. Black dots seem to be appearing in front of my eyes. Then all of a sudden, two men collapsed in front of me. They just seemed to crumble. Sergeant Horton's booming voice rang out, almost screaming, "Don't break ranks. Don't break ranks. Don't break those goddamn ranks," he continued to roar. "Boy! Step on those sonofabitches. Don't be squeamish. Step right on their goddamn faces. If they can't move out of the way, they deserve to die."

In a matter of minutes, more men fell, five, six, and in no time at all, the count had reached twenty. Sergeant Horton's voice rang out in a fevered pitch. He screeched, "Step on them, step on them, step on their heads." Then he started to bark commands. "To the rear, march ... march ... rip harsh ... rip harsh." Back and forth, we marched over the men's bodies. With our heavy boondockers, we stepped on their backs, their hands, their arms, and any part of their body that was in the line of march. Sergeant Horton, the sadistic SOB, was delighted, enthralled in his work. I prayed to the Lord to give me strength, to the saints, especially St. Anthony and St. Jude.

Finally, Sergeant Horton marched us around the fallen men and put us in a position that we were facing them. Then he ordered us to halt. The men appeared dead, but Sergeant Horton wasn't the least bit concerned. He started to talk to his platoon. He began slowly and softly. "Three men broke ranks to avoid stepping on these men's bodies. They deliberately disobeyed my orders, and they will be punished. I'm training men for war, for hell. When I give an order from now on, you'll carry it out or you'll be dead. At the end of any training day, any person or persons who foul up this outfit in any shape or form will pay a penalty, so you better execute my commands. Right now I have five men on my shit list. I hope I can stretch it to ten before we leave here."

Then he barked an order. "Now I want six volunteers for a shit detail." Before anyone could say a word, he pointed his finger at six men. "You, you, you, you, you, and you, come here. Drag these men up yonder and park their asses under the shade of those trees." He pointed to a clump of trees about 150 yards away. The supposed volunteers proceeded to grab the head and the feet of the unconscious marines and started to carry them off the field. Sergeant Horton screamed, "Drop those bastards," and they dropped them immediately. "Lookee here, you assholes, are you Greeks or are you Wops? None of you understand the King's English. I distinctly remember telling you to *drag* those bastards over yonder—drag them by their feet. I said nothing about carrying them. Now, if they're lying on their faces, then drag them on their faces. If they're lying on their backs, drag them on their backs." And with a growl he retorted, "Get them the hell out of here, now, on the double." The volunteers grabbed them by their feet and hurriedly dragged them to the shaded area. Many of the men came to and walked to the shaded area under their own power, much to the disgust of Sergeant Horton.

Sergeant Horton addressed the rest of his platoon. We were commanded to close ranks, cover down forty inches, back to breast. "Attention!" he screeched. "Right face. Forward harsh. A wan ... a reap ... a three four ... your left two ..." And the elimination procedure started all over again.

By five o'clock, there were only twenty-one of us left standing. Sergeant Horton had his kicks for today (we thought). After a ten-minute break, the order came to fall in again. Sick or not sick, you were marching home, and the sergeant made it very clear, "Any shithead that drops out now will be dragged on his ass to the barracks door." Believe me when I say no one passed out.

As we stood on the company street outside our barracks, Sergeant Horton again addressed his platoon. "I wasn't too satisfied with your first day of training. In fact, it was horse shit. If you're one of the men who crapped out, don't worry about it. You've had an experience. If you're one of the twenty-one men who didn't pass out, don't gloat over it. You're due for an experience. Tomorrow is another day, and we're going to do much better. Now I want the following men to step out of rank as I call their names." Loud and clear he shouted, "Ellison … DiLeo … Dixson … McCabe … Pascal … Ramos … Stevens."

They stood in front of the platoon, wondering why they were called. It didn't take any of us long to find out.

"You men are guilty of goofing off, and because of your negligence and indifferent attitudes, you have cost your platoon a two-hour night assignment. Two of you faked passing out today. How do I know? Well, that's why you're the assholes. The remainder of you shitheads had sloppy, shoddy sacks, and under your bunks there was dirt. It's too late for alibis. If it happens again, you all ride the range for a week. Now take off your shirts, strip down to your waist. You're going to run a gauntlet. The rest of you men, fall out and form two lines and face each other, and take off your belts." The men lined up thirty on each side.

Sergeant Horton continued speaking. "These seven men have cost you a night assignment. You are going to pay for their mistakes. You are going to suffer. They deserve to be punished. I want them punished. They are going to crawl on their knees before you, slowly. If they go too fast, they will go through again. Now as they pass, I want every man to strike them with your belt as hard as you can swing. If you are squeamish and don't strike him hard—and I'll be the judge—then you will go through that line three times in a row at a snail's pace. You hear me, boy? If you don't make an example of these men, then I'll break all your lily-white asses."

The first man lined up was Ellison. A tall boy, he had a kind of a nervous shit-eating grin on his young face. You could see he wanted to be brave and as he knelt down on all fours, he looked up at his fellow marines, apologizing with his eyes for causing them this problem. It was quiet, very quiet and still. Then he proceeded to crawl slowly through the line. Whack after whack rent the air, smash after smash the belts found their target. They struck his back, thrashed his head, and stung his neck and his ears. When he had reached the end of the line and he had paid his dues to his fellow men, Ellison stood up. His body was a mass of red welts, and his eyes were full of tears. Teardrops rolled down his cheeks. His young lace winced once or twice. He definitely had pain, but he did not cry. He acted like a true marine. Sergeant Horton told him to take his place at the end of the gauntlet.

As man after man went through that gauntlet line, they emerged as heroes to the troops. Although there were no words spoken, we communicated with our eyes. There were tears in the eyes of the men who went through the ordeal, but there was no crying. The Northerners were showing a Southerner that they could take all the shit he could hand out. Sure, they were hurt physically, but their pride was still intact.

Sergeant Horton's annoyance was clearly visible. I could see through this SOB now. We were being brainwashed. The sergeant was destroying individualism and there was no place to go, no place to hide, and no one to tell. Who in their right mind would believe your story?

CHAPTER VIII

Right after the gauntlet episode, we received our first mail-call. Again, Sergeant Horton had jurisdiction over the US mails. To the sergeant, letters were a waste, a sign of weakness. He didn't say it, but he implied it.

I was now deeply involved in trying to figure this bastard out. I watched his every move, I hung on his every word, and I could imitate his every call. He knew the Americans were soft and he was out to break this softness, this weakness, this crutch of democracy. I saw him in a different light. For the first time, I saw him for what he really was—a masterful teacher and a strict disciplinarian. I was going to play his game no matter what the cost, and I was still going to retain my own individualism; Lord God, give me strength.

Sergeant Horton informed us that no one would receive any more than two letters a day. He kept his word. Sometimes he would wave letters in front of your eyes, dangle them over your head, let you smell the perfume on the envelopes, show you who they were from, and then refuse to give them to you. All the time he was hoping, just hoping that you would make the wrong move, a hostile move, so he could take offense and give you some kind of a punishment. I was dying inside, but I showed no emotion on the outside. I was playing his game, but slowly and surely we were being indoctrinated—indoctrinated to his way of thinking. After all, it was his bat, his ball, and his game. We accepted things more readily; there was less complaining. Everything he said, you did without questioning it. Like he told us on the first night that we were there, "I'm your god. When I say do, you'll do, and when I say shit, you'll shit." It was a dog-eat-dog existence, and if he said "kill," believe me, you'd kill.

I received packages from home from family, from neighbors, and at one time I had eight packages waiting for me to pick up from the main area. The post office never delivered mail or packages to the boondocks. Someone picked up the mail and DIs would sort it out themselves, but no one received more than two letters a day. At least in our platoon that was the way first-class mail was handled. Packages were handled differently. If you received a package from home, then your DI would hand you a pick-up slip from the post office, you would walk five miles to the main post office, pick up your package, never open it, and carry it back to your DI.

Each night after training, Sergeant Horton would call me into his office. Sitting in his chair, he would look up at me with those slanty, beady eyes of his and blurt out in that gruff, graveled voice, "Well, boy! You got some more goodies again. In fact, you have quite a few of them, but you're going to pick them up one at a time, boy!" Then he would hand me a PO slip and instruct me never to open it under penalty of a court-martial. I would return with the package intact and hand it over to him. I would then stand at attention with the sweat pouring down my face and watch the shit-eating grin on the sergeant's face as he opened the packages. "Lookie here, lookie here," he would say as he opened the box. His left eye would look up at me in a sort of a squint, and with his head at a tilt, many a time our eyes would meet. In a raised voice, he would holler, "Don't look at me like that, boy! Get that look off your face." Through these little actions I knew he was reading me loud and clear. Without so much as a word, he knew I held him in contempt. I also knew that someday this hell would end and if I ever got the upper hand, I'd make him squirm. I'd make him squawk. I'd make him shit square bricks. But now he was the boss, and in a gloating, raspy voice he would tell me in his slow Southern drawl, "You kin folks make mighty fine cookies," or "You mammy's cookies done hit the spot." From the open package, he took anything and everything he wanted. From Vicks VapoRub to Bengay, from toilet articles to personal gifts, and from cookies to candy. He was a real thief, but to clear his conscience he would say that he was only doing his duty.

Some nights when the take was small, he would send me down to the post office again. Twenty miles of walking, just being on the road was a living hell, for your right hand was always in the air. Up and down it went like a railroad crossing gate. You just didn't salute the officers, but also their wives, their cars, their kids, their goddamn dogs. These superior people, these bigots. Was it worth fighting a war for the likes of them? Were they worth one man's life? Parris Island was a rude awakening in more ways than one.

Once on the sidewalks, you ran into more problems. Officers were as thick as flies. They came at you in all directions, old officers and young officers with their wives. I could hear them snicker as I saluted their shitbird husbands. I was beginning to hate everybody's guts, but I was also learning to discipline myself in little ways, rationing myself to five cigarettes a day, making myself enjoy the chores like washing clothes by hand and standing fire watch. Even cleaning latrines with a toothbrush was not going to dampen my spirits.

Letters were arriving every day now and although I was only receiving a few a day, my mother kept me well-informed with the home-front news. She informed me as to the changes that were taking place, notably the meat and sugar shortages, the planned shortages, the rationing stamps, and the high cost of living. I wrote back that my needs were few and that I would send her home forty dollars of my fifty-dollar-a-month pay. When they took out the premium for my $8,000 insurance policy, I received thirty-five to forty dollars per month to live on. Again I disciplined myself by denying buying anything except soap and toothpaste. I never wrote my family about the hardships of training, and I'm sure they were under the impression that I was having a good summer vacation, but I did inform them to stop sending me packages.

I also received a letter from a Sue Cole. Sue was a good friend of mine from the office where I had worked in New York City. She informed me that I had won twenty-five dollars in the company's monthly drawing for servicemen. She was elated over the fact that she had picked my card out of the bowl, and told me outright that I owed her a dinner date when I came home on furlough. Sue was a nice girl, a good-looking girl with a willowy figure and as graceful as a swan. She was a very popular girl at the office and in her pretty, flowery dresses, she would flutter around the office like a butterfly. She was the news reporter of the office and out of the office. Anything that was worth knowing, Sue could tell you about it. She always had a friend who knew, or her father who told her so. Her father was an executive with the New York Central Railroad Company and according to Sue, everybody knew her daddy, James Barton Cole. She was a Westchester girl and resided in Harrison, New York. She wasn't working for the money, but it was something to do. It brought her to the big city every day, and she met her friends for lunch. She didn't work hard and she met interesting people. She liked it and it was only a temporary thing with her.

She was a good friend and school chum of my friend Kappy, and that's how I became acquainted with her. In her letter, she mentioned that Kappy was living in a little town near Fort Benning, Georgia, and that her husband was now an officer in the United States Army, Lt. Gregory C. Madigan. From this information, I knew she was very much in touch with Kappy and although I held no grudges, I was not about to disclose any business of my private life nor did I want to hear any information from anyone else's private life. I threw the letter on the bed. Then I picked it up, tore it up, and threw it into the trash can. This letter upset me. I never remembered sending Sue my address, and now I definitely had no intentions of answering her letter, at least for now.

The first week of training passed, and Sunday being the Lord's day, it was still a work day in the Marine Corps. However, they did allow us to go to the church of our choice. Panos and Corr were atheists—at least they said they were—and they remained home cleaning latrines while the rest of the men took off for church service. Just getting away from this area was a health tonic, and we never enjoyed a Mass more in our lives. In fact, we were wishing it would never end, but it did, and in no time at all they had us washing clothes and cleaning gear. For Sunday dinner we had turkey, and I could have sworn they cooked the turkey without plucking the feathers, for I got more feathers than turkey.

In the afternoon, Corporal Howard took us to the wash area to clean the grease off our rifles and bayonets. In one area the tubs contained soapy water, in another rinse water. It was some ordeal, and we had to put them through this operation at least three times before they looked clean. The operation was time-consuming, and in the next two months you would still be cleaning the grease off your rifle.

Sergeant Horton was still full of surprises. We were kept so busy with physical training, close-order drill, school exercises, fire watches, guard duty, head details, field days, and studying the parts of our rifles that we didn't have time to breathe. The sergeant would never let us relax. He would call on us at any hour of the day or night for shit details, or to take us on a moonlight walk, or to just wake us out of a deep sleep. He was a bastard and he always had us on edge. One morning he woke us up at 2:00 a.m. Any time he came into the barracks, he was miserable. He was like a curse, always causing pain and unhappiness. This particular morning he outdid himself, and that took some doing. On went the lights and he screamed at the top of his lungs, "Hit the deck! Hit the deck, goddamnit, and be outside in one minute for roll call," and he continued, "Wear nothing but your skivvy drawers and your boondockers."

Following his orders, we immediately fell out for roll call in front of our barracks. Once the call was taken, the sergeant bellowed, "Right face! Forward, march," and we headed in the direction of the boondocks.

The night was very dark and the air seemed very damp, almost misty. Even through the blackness, Sergeant Horton knew where he was going. He knew every inch of this rock with his eyes closed. We marched over the sand dunes and into the gullies and as we traveled along at a quick pace, the sand was building up in our shoes. The sergeant was calling for a cadence count every three or four minutes, and young, strong voices ripped the air with a "one, two, three, four" at their NCO's command. "Louder, louder!" he barked, and again he ordered a cadence count. "One, two, three, four," his platoon screamed in unison.

On and on we marched into territory that was not familiar, and then the terrain became swampy and wet. I could feel the water seeping into my shoes, mingling with the sand. It was creating friction between my heel and the shoe. It was most uncomfortable. And then, without notice, Sergeant Horton shouted a command to his troops: "Platoon, halt, one, two." Everything was quiet. It was pitch-black, and we were stuck in the middle of nowhere.

Sergeant Horton, who always acted like God in front of his platoon, couldn't resist the temptation to change night into day, and he accomplished this feat in a matter of minutes. Parked in four different places in the swamp area were marine jeeps. They were set there by god and his motley crew. One at a time he started the engines and turned on the high-beam lights. It created an eerie setting in this dismal swamp with its large trees and hanging moss. They lurked like monsters in the distance. Yes, the props were good, and the water at our feet reflected the lights into the trees, thus adding to this eerie creation of Sergeant Horton.

We were on stage now and basking in the limelight. Any way we turned, the lights would hit us in the eye. We were surrounded by them. Sergeant Horton, our tormenter, marched back and forth in front of us. He screamed obscenities at us. Then, with his swagger stick slapping against his pants leg, he addressed his outfit. "Men, we're on a long night maneuver, and from this day forward, we are going to have more night patrols besides your day training, so get used to it. The one we are on now is called a 'Mosquito Patrol,' and in any patrol or scout exercise, the idea is to find the enemy. Tonight we are aiding the enemy with the lights and helping him find you." With this remark, his mouth curled up in a sort of a sneer. "This is a kind of an endurance test. Any time a mosquito bites you and you move, your platoon will stand out here another half-hour, and anyone guilty of moving will go through the gauntlet." He then proceeded to bring the platoon to attention.

The first fifteen minutes wasn't bad, but then it became unbearable. The mosquitoes buzzed in your ear, they bit you on the lip, your neck, your back, your legs, and your arms. It was mosquito picnic time, and Sergeant Horton was having a ball. You tried your damnedest not to move. You thought of things that happened a million years ago. You thought of home, the fun Mull and Beau were having; you were playing your dreams right on this goddamn swamp. God help me, offer it up for the poor souls. St. Anthony, help me. Jesus Christ, kill this bastard.

Sergeant Horton caught eleven men moving, and we stayed there until five o'clock in the morning. It was one living hell. When we started to march, I could feel the numbness right up to my thighs. Once we were back at the barracks, there was no time for anything. Everyone was just one big itch. Our training day had begun, and the first thing on the agenda was making the eleven men run through the gauntlet. Sergeant Horton supervised this job and then retired to his quarters. Corporal Howard marched us to chow, and the one thing we needed today was joe—old black joe—and we needed lots of it.

This morning in school we learned how to strip our .03 rifle. We had to know every little part of this weapon, and before we were through we would be able to put it together blindfolded.

Sergeant Horton rejoined his platoon at 1100 Navy time (11 a.m.). We fell out in two ranks. "Platoon, attention!" ordered Sgt. Horton, then "Dress right dress …cover down forty inches back to breast. Ready … front. I'm holding a personal inspection this morning. If I tell you to step out, then you step out."

He then proceeded to approach every one of his men. He stood in front of them, looking up at them, looking down at them, looking into their eyes, scrutinizing them from head to toe, examining their very souls. If you passed he would continue on, sidestepping to the next man, and if he said step out, you were in trouble—big trouble.

After going through his men, he had fourteen of his men pulled from the ranks. He brought them to the front of the platoon. "Every one of these men are guilty of not shaving, and therefore we will proceed to shave them … the marine way." He had two razors and both had dull blades in them. He picked up a handful of sand and rubbed it on the recruit's face, scratching him up good. Then with the dry razor, he proceeded to shave him. He brought the razor close to the skin and came down hard and fast. The young marine winced in pain as a little trickle of blood appeared on his face. "You'll live, shitbird, but the next time I'll cut your goddamn throat," and he then proceeded to finish the job. Up and down he went with that razor, not missing one hair and pulling it out by the roots. He finally finished shaving the first man, but the next thirteen were shaved by boots supervised by him. The recruits were so anxious to please their master that they were crueler than he was—they butchered their own buddies. Every one of the men looked like they were shaved with sandpaper.

Once that chore was finished, he had other things on his mind. It had come to his attention that two men in his platoon had not taken a bath in a week. "This I will not tolerate. Tonight at 2000 hours [8:00 p.m.] Private Fiber and Private Gallenhurst will get a public bath. All members of this platoon will either participate or attend. And if anyone else has not taken a bath, you can believe me after tonight's performance you will. I'll shit you not.

"Another thing has been brought to my attention. Two men in this platoon have conspired against me. Imagine, two men notifying their pappies that I've been a little rough on their lily-white asses. Well, I'm not changing my methods or tactics for any Northern shitheads. Out here I'm law," he screamed. "Out here I'm god. Private Navarro and Private Clovis, step out." He then addressed the men. "After training tonight, you'll report to the galley and you'll ride that hot freaking range until midnight every night, and you'll ride it till your ass sucks buttermilk. Ya heah me?" he screeched.

"Yes, sir," they quickly replied.

Without batting an eyelash, he called two more men out of the ranks. "Private Ralston and Private Pershing have another problem." He then went on to relate, "That strange odor you smell in your barracks is not a skunk; it's piss. Yes, piss. These men have been urinating in their sacks every night. Someone told them if the training gets too tough then all you have to do is to piss in your sacks and the Marine Corps will give you a medical discharge." Then dropping his voice, he said softly, "Son, we haven't even begun to train as yet. But the marines don't want your kind. You're the assholes that give up the ship. You're the shitbirds that can't take an order. You're the garbage that when it comes down to the nitty-gritty, you just can't take it. I put both of you in for a court-martial, but until your case comes up, you'll stay right here. As of now, you'll move your bunks out of the barracks and you'll place them between our barracks and the next-door barracks. Your mattresses have been confiscated as evidence. You will sleep on the springs. You have your blankets, and if they are ever pissed on, I'll have you soak them in your pail and you'll rinse them in your pail, and by God you'll drink that piss. In fact, you'll be the first two guys that ever drowned in their own piss." And looking at them in disgust, he blurted, "I'll shit you not." And without so much as a nod, he took off and entered the barracks.

Corporal Howard was now in charge, and for the next two hours we had close-order drill. And if I must say so myself, the platoon looked sharp. No one had to run the gauntlet that evening.

CHAPTER IX

As we entered our barracks from the hard day of training, I noticed we had three new faces waiting to join our platoon. These men weren't exactly new recruits; they had previously been with another platoon. Unfortunately, they had sickness and they had to report to sick bay (hospital), and they had missed more than three days of training. In the Marine Corps, if you lost three successive days of training, and then you automatically were put back into another platoon when you were released from sick bay. This was the story on these new men: all of them had been discharged from the hospital today, and they had been on the island for at least a month. They were now ordered back to duty and to continue their training.

Two of these men were rebels, and the other recruit was from Philadelphia. These two rebels were the first Southerners in our platoon. Sergeant Horton almost jumped over the moon when Bob Humpfrey said he was from Timberlane, Georgia. Timberlane was a little town located deep in the Okefenokee Swamp of Georgia.

When two Southerners get together, their speech is not too bad; but when four Southerners start a discussion, their drawls become so heavy and thick that they tangle into a ball of twine. They became most difficult to understand, and even the most refined ones become loud, crude, and sometimes vulgar. We Northerners looked at them in amazement. We couldn't understand them, but from their actions they were having a helluva time. They hooted and they howled; they slapped hands and backs and roared with laughter over the simplest of things. We were glad they were having a good time, for it got Sergeant Horton off our backs temporarily.

Bob Humpfrey, the lad from Timberlane, Georgia, wasn't a big man and you could hardly call him physical. He stood around five feet eight inches and would be considered a feather merchant in the eyes of Sergeant Horton. And when he shook your hand—well, it was like holding a washcloth floating around in a bathtub, and just as supple. Now his slow drawl and quick wit immediately made him a favorite with the troops and despite his being a Southerner, his personality came through loud and strong. He reminded you of a country doctor or a traveling preacher. Every night before bedtime or taps, Preacher Bob would make his rounds. Stopping at each bunk, he would talk to each man. In his slow-ass Georgia drawl, he would ask questions, tell a joke, give advice, shower praise, or give solace with a few kind words. It was uncanny how this man could read your mood. He was kind, and he was friendly and a highly intelligent person. We overheard that his father was a doctor, but most of us were not interested in his family tree—especially my friends and I—but we did accept him as a friend, and later on a special friend.

Alfonso Calvin Moore was a tall, gangling Southern lad from Goldsboro, North Carolina. He was a typical Southerner, and he had the look of a farm boy who would come from a hick town. You could picture this guy in overalls wearing a large straw hat, pitching hay. He was that type. Sergeant Horton always referred to him as "Mo, that long drink of piss." But Moore was not the innocent boy he portrayed. Far from it. He was the most out-and-out rebel that I have ever met. North, east, south, west, they were all the same to Massa Mo, as he liked to be called. In Goldsboro, North Carolina, he was a whiskey rum runner. His job was delivering illegal whiskey all over the state of South Carolina. He boasted that he made more than a hundred dollars a day. He was the proud possessor of a souped-up car, and he would show us pictures of it like someone would show pictures of their girlfriend. There was Massa Mo in front of the car, Massa Mo in back of the car, Massa Mo in the car. Yes, he did love that car, almost as much as he loved himself.

The only reason Alfonso Moore was in the Marine Corps was because the authorities had shot the rear tires out of his car in a wild chase in Wilson, North Carolina. He was arrested, tried, and convicted of bootlegging corn whiskey and sentenced to ten years in federal prison. Fortunately, he had money, and it cost him $12,000 to have his lawyers overturn the jail sentence. They promised the judge that if they let him off, he would join the US Marines Corps and fight for his country and die for it—according to Mo, that's the way the script read. Well, he didn't go to jail, but he regretted it now. He said it would have been a lot easier, and he would still have his money.

While at the hospital in the main area, he had a good thing going, and he made a lot of money. He was the only marine who wore three money belts at one time. He had been at the hospital for six weeks, and it broke his heart to come back to active duty. While at the hospital, he would sneak out at night, go to the post exchange, and buy boxes and boxes of candy. Then he would visit barrack after barrack, platoon after platoon, and sell his merchandise. Five-cent bars of candy he sold for a quarter and fifteen-cent boxes of ice cream he would sell for fifty cents. He was cleaning up. He also sold soda, cigarettes, and cigars, anything for a profit. All these items were forbidden fruit for boots. He was some hustler, and he would always be a hustler. They said he was in the hospital for falling out of a tree, but word was passed around that four sergeants beat Mo for selling candy and sweets to their platoons. He was beaten so severely he almost died. Mo never admitted it, but he never denied it either. He would shrug it off as the fortunes of war. Sergeant Horton warned Moore once, "If you ever sell one candy bar to any of my men, shitbird, I'll see to it that you have the best military funeral this side of the Mason-Dixon line." And the way he said it, you knew he meant it.

Pat Monahan wasn't just an ordinary boot, and he wasn't just an ordinary Irishman either. Pat was an ace news reporter for the *Philadelphia Inquirer*, one of the leading papers in the state of Pennsylvania. He wanted to cover the war news for the US Marines in the Pacific Theater as a war correspondent. To get this assignment, he had to go through boot camp with the marine recruits to qualify. Although he was only twenty-nine years old, a comparatively young man, he was encountering all sorts of difficulties trying to complete his basic training. He had just been released from the hospital after spending a month there for complete physical exhaustion.

He was married to a pretty Irish lass named Patricia Anne and her nickname was also "Pat." Sissie, his three-year-old daughter, and Ronnie, his four-year-old son, rounded out the family. Pat was proud of his family and displayed them in photographs all around his bunk.

Pat was a good-looking man of medium height and a good muscular build. With his deep blue eyes and his neatly trimmed crew cut, he could have passed for Jack Armstrong, the all-American boy. However, despite his physical attributes, he was far from an aggressive person. He had a very apologetic nature and was forever putting himself down. I think his flunking out the first time he went through this boot training had a lot to do with his apologies. He was unsure of himself. This bothered Sergeant Horton at certain times, and when it irked him, he would blurt out angrily, "For Christ's sake, do me a favor, man, and say, 'shit!'" But Pat never cursed and he never swore. You would have sworn that he was a devoted Irish Catholic, but again he would fool you. Pat was a Protestant and I, being a Catholic and half-Irish, always thought of this denomination as black Protestants. Again, Pat fooled you. He was whitest guy in our platoon. Because of his humble nature, the men found him easy to talk to, and easy to listen to, and everyone was rooting for Pat to pass his basic test.

I remembered how often my Catholic-reared mother said hostile things about people of other religions. It wasn't always nice. In fact, she could be vicious. In her defense, however, bitterness from her widowhood and the era prompted a hostile reaction in general. The familial sentiment and era predisposed children to a prejudiced attitude, the kind of which youngsters overhear when the parents talk and gossip. Beliefs are adopted as their own, without conscious examination. I was guilty of such.

Having been raised a Catholic, because my mother insisted, and an altar boy, several occasions prompted me to be upset as a youth. I had been verbally threatened and physically abused by a nun, and had arguments with my older sisters, who thought nothing of yanking me out of the lineup to bat during important baseball games to have me to sing in the choir. But then again, the priests who ran the boys' park and coached baseball and football were good as gold.

No incident would hit home in shining a light on my religious prejudice like my friendship with Pat. I had been schooled that all Protestants were "fallen Catholics"—bad, morally corrupt people. I saw firsthand now that was malarkey! I knew then how my religious belief had hardened my heart against good, upright people of noble character. I was shocked, shaken to the core. That moment I made a conscious decision to give people a chance. My experience alone would later determine whether or not hostility or intolerance on my part would be warranted.

At 2000 hours (8:00 p.m.) that evening, Sergeant Horton reappeared on the scene. He was neatly appareled in starched khaki, scarf, and barracks cap. He also was wearing his ribbons. All the men looked at him in awe. Despite his temperament, vulgar expressions, and nasty disposition, Sergeant Horton was one helluva-looking marine in his salty uniform; and with his reddish-bronze complexion, he looked like something etched out of metal. His appearance commanded respect, and from the glint in his eye, he demanded it. "We have some unfinished business to attend to tonight, men," he shouted in his best Southern drawl. Everyone knew what he was referring to. "Tonight, men, we're giving a physical demonstration in personal hygiene. Cleanliness is next to godliness." Then raising his voice in a loud command, he roared, "Private Fiber and Private Gallenhurst, step forward, front and center." The two young recruits came forward immediately and stood at attention before their superior.

Pvt. Harold Fiber was a rather small young man. He had come from a small farming town called Pinecreek, located near Schenectady, New York. Harold was the youngest boy in our platoon. He had just celebrated his seventeenth birthday three weeks ago, and looking at him from any angle, you would swear he was only fourteen years old. His face was so youthful-looking he appeared as a boy. This was the first time he had ever been away from home. Harold was a nice-looking lad, clean cut, quiet, and well-mannered. He only spoke when he was spoken to, and even then you had to talk to him directly, for he was a shy boy, and his answers were always "yes, sir" or "no, sir." He was no conversationalist and seemed to avoid prolonged conversations because of his shyness. He kept to himself all the time. In fact, you'd hardly know he was around. He never mingled with the men, and he never played cards. No, he never even watched a card game.

Every night Harold would write one letter home, and then he would take out his Bible and read and read and read. Many times he would hide his head in his pillow or just stare into space for hours. This boy wasn't just longing for home—he was pining for home. He reminded me of a young puppy, a lost puppy, a whining puppy. He was so homesick that he was dying from loneliness.

In every society, group, club, or organization, wherever men congregate, be it the White House in Washington DC or the Boy Scouts in Kansas City, there is a certain segment of men known as a clique who become the *in* crowd. This group of men are good men, but the majority of them are so wrapped up in themselves and so self-centered that they never see other people's problems. They start rumors, and then the rumors spread into gossip, and the gossip could be malicious and detrimental to one's character; but this does not worry the clique, for they are the only ones who count. Sometimes, unfortunately, the clique contains the best men and the smartest men in their organization, but nevertheless, in all places these are dangerous men. It is most difficult to recognize these men immediately, especially in a new organization. They're the collaborators, the ass kissers, the brown noses, the bigots, the loudmouths, the "who I am, where I came from, where I'm going, and what are you going to do about it." Perceptive people can see through them, so temporarily they avoid the strong and the knowledgeable people. They do this by isolating them, always keeping them in the minority, thus making this group ineffective. Now they can work, and their targets are the masses, the ignorant, the meek, and the weak. They dictate company policy; they are the organization within the organization.

Sergeant Horton, a master of psychology and an expert predictor in the behavior of human nature, dictated his orders at the beginning of our training period. He also ordered us to do as he said under threat of severe penalties. He intimidated us. He also planted seeds into the minds of others, and he knew from past experience, as sure as hell, that there were men in his platoon who wanted to make points, who would do anything to get on the good side of him. He throws out a few crumbs (if anyone disobeys my orders, let me know) and they bite. Oh, how they bite! An ass kisser is born, a brown nose is created, and an informer is now in our midst. A few more words of flattery and this informer will sell his soul.

Now Sergeant Horton issues orders upon orders. Don't do this and don't do that. He now knows that this select group will see that his orders are carried out. They become the watchdogs of the platoon. They notice every little thing in detail. Nothing escapes their eyes or their ears. Hitler was using this plan effectively for years, but it could never happen here. "Bullshit." It was happening. These informers had turned in eight men. There would be more.

Sergeant Horton was proud of himself. Not that he had respect for these men, for he didn't, but his job would be easier. There would be no trouble now, no interference. His word was law. These bastards, these informers would now squeal on their own mother. They were completely indoctrinated.

My so-called friend, Pvt. Forrest Corr, was the ringleader of this group. I would listen to him speak out against these men, first softly, then openly, but I ignored him completely. I too was indoctrinated at an early age by my grandparents to "mind my own business."

Corr went to others who listened. He was an organizer, a good speaker, intelligent; he soon had a group, and they dictated company policy. He also had a physical group behind him, and they enforced his policy. Soon they were buzzing the corporal, who in turn informed the sergeant, who made things happen. Looking back in retrospect, these men were probably guilty, but under the circumstances they should have had a chance to adapt. Corporal punishment was not the answer. It could have been handled differently, but it wasn't.

Pvt. Andrew Gallenhurst, like Private Fiber, was also young and immature. He had just turned eighteen years old, and he was no introvert. Far from it. Andy was a big, outgoing lad. He reminded you of a playful large St. Bernard dog. He forced himself on people. To look for attention, he would play practical jokes. He was just a big kid who needed guidance and understanding, but in this platoon he found neither. Here, he was ridiculed and unwanted. If he volunteered for a card game, the men told him to screw or "beat it, kid." He was told he couldn't do this and he couldn't do that. He became the eight ball of the platoon, and when anything was screwed up, Private Gallenhurst was blamed. He was the scapegoat for everything, taking more verbal abuse, more beatings, riding more ranges, and receiving more shit details than any ten marines, and he had only been here two weeks. The days weren't long enough for Andy to complete his many punishments and penalties. This young man was either coming or going to some shit detail, and through it all he would always laugh, perplexing Sergeant Horton no end. The kid had a perpetual shit-eating grin.

Whenever Private Gallenhurst had a spare moment or a free night, he would flop out on his bunk and through sheer exhaustion, he would be asleep in a matter of minutes. Sometimes he would sleep right through till reveille the next morning. Private Corr and his group reported that this man sleeps with his clothes on and does not take a bath. Never weighing the circumstances against the evidence, they convicted him of not taking a bath.

Sergeant Horton, eyeing the two boots, then called for volunteers who would give these men a bath and teach them a lesson. Private Corr and nine of his buddies stepped forward immediately. The sergeant was delighted with the response. Looking at his squinty eyes, they were dancing with joy. You could see he was elated, and he cried out in glee, "Lookie here, lookie here! We have to do this thing right. Now get three mops and three street brooms and a couple of pails, two bars of Octagon soap, and two tent ropes." Quickly Corr's group ran to get the necessary equipment and just as quickly they returned, screaming and screeching like a pack of wild Indians. They clamored for action and Sergeant Horton, seeing their eagerness, spurred them on. "What are you waiting for, men? They're all yours."

The majority of us looked on in amazement as the men grabbed the two recruits and carried them off bodily to the showers. The two men kicked and squirmed, but to no avail as the men almost ripped their arms from their sockets. Punches were flying in all directions as the younger men fought for their dignity. Once inside the shower, the two men were put on their feet. Private Fiber was bleeding from the nose and the mouth. Private Gallenhurst was none the worse for wear.

Once Sergeant Horton arrived, he ordered the two men to disrobe. Private Gallenhurst did so immediately, but Private Fiber just stood there defiantly. The sergeant was outraged. He did not give the order again. Instead he told his troops to rip them off, and amid screams and screeches that reached to the high heavens, Private Fiber was as naked as a jaybird in a matter of minutes. Sergeant Horton ordered Private Fiber hog-tied. Twice Fiber broke away and twice they smashed that frail body on the slippery, hard concrete floor. Then they pushed the men toward the showers. Turning the water on full blast, they swabbed the men with the soapy mops. Everywhere and anywhere those mops tangled with those young bodies. Once soaped, they took the push brooms and completed the washing job. Then they pushed the men in line with the shower sprays and doused them with ice-cold water. The washing job was complete, and we returned to our barracks. It was quite a night.

With the arrival of the new recruits, our platoon was now up to full strength, sixty-five strong young men who were eager to learn, anxious to fight, and willing to die (if necessary) to rid the world of dictators and tyranny. How ironic.

The next phase of our training was already being discussed and planned by a most competent, most reliable, and most capable instructor, who also was the most compelling and intolerant bastard who ever marched "in this land that God forgot, where the sand is fourteen inches deep and the sun is scorching hot."—Sergeant Robert E. Horton

CHAPTER X

As the weeks wore on, the men in our platoon became so toughened to the physical routine that three-hour marches under the hot sun didn't affect us at all. Everyone seemed to be trying so hard that Sergeant Horton had to scrutinize us to find fault. Then we started working out with our rifles and bayonets, and it was a brand new ball game. It wasn't the additional ten pounds that we were carrying that seemed to cause the problem, but it was the new commands with the rifle while we were doing close-order drill that made the men commit mistakes. Sergeant Horton, never a tolerant man, screamed and hollered continually. "You don't know your left from your right, you don't know shit from beans, you don't know your ass from a hole." Over and over again, he would berate us. It would go on for hours. At the end of the day, half the platoon would run the gauntlet, but each day we were getting a little better.

And when we finally became good at our drill formations, Sergeant Horton found something else to bitch about. It came to his attention that the men were not hitting their rifles hard enough, and not in unison. Back and forth we would march as he would screech, "Left shoulder arms. Hit those stocks louder. Harder." Then "Right shoulder arms. Louder. Hit them harder." This went on for hours, and after a while your hands became sore and numb, so sore that it was an effort to hold your rifle, let alone pound the steel with your bare hands.

There was never compassion in Sergeant Horton's makeup. He was dissatisfied with the way we hit our rifles, and he did something about it. In the corner of the parade field, there were around a dozen cement blocks, two feet square. We often wondered what these blocks were for. Well, we soon found out. Sergeant Horton marched us before these blocks one day and called out fifteen names. He then proceeded to tell us about the stones. "The stones you see yonder are called praying stones. That's right, boy! They are praying stones, and when you pray on these rocks, you have direct contact with the Lord and you learn fast. Fifteen of you men are not hitting your weapons as you should. You need practice, and here is where you'll get it. I want all of you men to kneel in front of these blocks—that's why they're called praying stones."

The fifteen men proceeded to do as the sergeant said. When all of them were in the kneeling position, he directed them to raise their hands above their heads and when he counted one, they were to smash that rock in front of them with the palms of their hands. Each time he counted, they were to hit that rock with all their might. "The rest of you men, I want you to observe, for tomorrow, if you happen to be here, and then you will hit that praying stone like a tom-tom two hundred times. I'm not shitting you one bit." Then he had the men beat that rock one hundred times. Most of their hands were bleeding when they were finished, but we went right back to marching again and we didn't leave the area until it was dark. Private Moore, Private Fiber, and Private Gallenhurst rode the range that night for dropping their rifles, and besides were ordered to sleep with the rifle for a week.

In addition to the marching and the barracks routine, we were learning other things as well—namely, how to properly shoot a pistol and a rifle, how to use the bayonet, and hand-to-hand combat training. The vast majority of the marines in training were physical men. Teaching these men the finer points on how to kill a man either with a bullet, a rifle butt, a bayonet, knife, or hand-to-hand combat training came easily to most of us. We adapted to this training easily. It was like playing football: the more you practiced, the better you became at the sport. We became as agile as cats, and all the men gave 110 percent, especially with Sergeant Horton standing close by, hands on hips, observing everyone with those squinty green eyes, watching each individual perform and taking mental notes. He never missed a trick.

At night, after evening chow, we would practice snapping in on our rifles. In a nearby field, they had a course set up for snapping-in exercises. Little white crosses with dots in the middle decked the surrounding area. From a distance, it looked like a cemetery. On these crosses you would line up the sights of your .03 rifle in this manner. First you would attach the rifle sling to your arm and adjust it to a comfortable position. Then, standing about twenty feet from your target, you would take the position you wanted to shoot from—sitting, kneeling, or prone. Then you would proceed to line up your target through your sights. The sling helps to steady the rifle and helps to take up the recoil when you fire it. There are two sights on the rifle, the front sight and the rear peep sight. First you blacken the sights with a match. This prevents reflection of light from the sights. Light causes the front sight to blur, thereby interfering with your aim. Now you're ready for sighting and aiming. You align the sights by bringing the tip of the front sight to the exact center of the peep sight. In combat, when using open (or battle) sights, you bring the tip of the front sight to the center of the open sight and level or flush with its top edge. The bull's-eye or silhouette should be aligned with the bottom edge or just touching (sitting on) the top edge of the front sight. Your eye must focus while aiming directly on the target. You know your eye is focused when the target appears sharp and clear. If your vision becomes blurred, take your rifle down and start over again. You should rest your cheek against the stock of the rifle. This helps to hold the rifle and brings your eye near the cocking piece. By doing this, it makes the aim uniform and rapid. Now you hold your breath. Breathing moves the body, thus disturbing aim. Now you're ready to squeeze the trigger. This is what you're practicing for. A quick pull or a yank of the trigger deranges it, therefore squeezing the trigger is absolutely necessary for good shooting. By a slow, steady squeeze, the alignment of the rifle will remain fixed. Everything is now ready. With the second joint of your forefinger, you take up the slack of the trigger. Then with sights properly aligned on the bull's-eye, you take a deep breath, exhale part, and hold the balance in a natural manner. Now gradually increase the pressure on the trigger until the rifle fires.

If you had squeezed the trigger correctly, the moment of fire is not known. That's the purpose of snapping in, to get the feel of your weapon, to know it, to love it. This is your baby, your protector. Someday this rifle will be your lifeline. You point it at people to kill them. There is no joking with this weapon. That's why even when you're snapping in, you call your shots. In one more week, we would be going to the rifle range, and you had to know your weapon inside and outside by then. All marine boots spent at least two hours a day snapping in. This was the time to learn all about your rifle, and no one can say they didn't try.

The next morning after chow (breakfast), we started out on a routine training session. It was a training session in water discipline and forced marches. We did not take any canteens of water with us. For the next forty-eight hours, we would be either marching or standing on our feet for at least thirty-two of those hours.

Ever since the night we spent in the swamps, I had developed an infection on my left foot. It resembled eczema at the start, and I treated it with foot powder. It itched and it itched, and then it spread rapidly. My friends thought it to be poison ivy or poison oak or blood poison. They told me to report to sick bay. I refused because I didn't want to be set back into another platoon at this last stage of training. Just the thought of repeating this training spurred me on. It would be worth a foot to get the hell out of this place. The sores were seeping, and I wore two pairs of socks to protect it. This particular morning it was bad, so bad that the itching turned into a throbbing pain, and it was beginning to affect my walk.

The day ahead was scheduled not just to work, but to work overtime. As soon as we had begun to march, sweat was pouring from our heads like an overflowing waterfall, streaming down onto our faces, creating a burning sensation in our eyes and tickling our noses. As it passed our lips, pearly beads of sweat would penetrate our mouths and a sour liquid similar to vinegar would awaken our taste buds. Our mouths became dry and our saliva became thick, and we longed for water, a cool drink of water. Our uniforms were saturated with sweat from our bodies, and the green dungarees were black from the wetness. Sergeant Horton stood under a tree, sounding out orders loud and clear.

The first man to fall in the sand was Pvt. Pat Monahan. Sergeant Horton ran to his platoon like a vulture pouncing on a dead carcass. This is what he was waiting for—this is what he was expecting. The first man to fall started a chain reaction, and in no time at all fifteen men were down and Sergeant Horton was screaming and cursing, "Don't break those ranks! Step on their heads, step on their ass, don't break goddamn ranks!" And we marched on top of them, on any part of the bodies that was in the line of march—their faces, hands, back, legs, and feet. Sergeant Horton ordered us to step on them, and we did what we were told to do.

For six consecutive hours, Sergeant Horton marched us in that sand, and it looked like the March of Bataan. The hot sun was beating down, and strewn all over the area were bodies of men who had fallen. No one was allowed in the shade, and no one was allowed any water. Now there were only seven of us remaining and the sergeant was going for a clean sweep, but the same group of men remained upright. Finally, in desperation, he put us through stationary double-time and just when it appeared as if we would all collapse, he ordered us to halt. Private Gallenhurst, the young recruit who received more shit details than anyone in the platoon, couldn't believe that he survived. The shit-eating grin was always present, and Sergeant Horton just shook his head in disbelief. He too couldn't believe Gallenhurst made it, but he didn't make any comment. But he did take a note of the men who survived the ordeal.

Hurriedly, he ordered the men to fall in and we headed back to the barracks. Our lips were so parched that they swelled up in the hot sun. Sergeant Horton marched us to a new area. He lined us up before four horse troughs and proceeded to fill them with water. Standing in front of the running water, he started to taunt us. "Look at that water, you shitheads. Boy! How nice and cool it is." Then filling his canteen, he would drink in front of us, telling us all the time how refreshing the water was. For almost an hour, we stood in front of those troughs. The water overflowed onto the dirt street, and as we watched the small trickles of water aimlessly creeping steadily forward in our direction, we unconsciously became aware that our tongues were circling and licking our parched lips. Then Sergeant Horton, walking continually up and down the street, observing our every movement, seemingly trying to penetrate our very minds, called us to attention in a loud, clear voice, "Listen, you pigs. When I dismiss you, you have five minutes to drink and get back in formation. Ya heah me!" Then stepping aside, he screamed, "Platoon dismissed. Drink, you pigs." And we ran screaming for the overflowing horse troughs. God, it was a sight to behold: men throwing themselves right into the basinlike tubs, others kneeling and dunking their heads in and out of the water. God! How good it felt, and how sweet it tasted. We would have lingered there for an hour, but we were only given five minutes. Still, it was the sweetest five minutes I've ever spent anywhere.

When we returned to the barracks that night, my left foot was so inflamed and swollen, so terribly sore and tender, that I had extreme difficulty removing my shoe and socks. It was painfully sore and ugly to look at. My friends were now very concerned, and Joe Setzer insisted that I shouldn't wait any longer but to report to sick bay now. Their concern frightened me, and I almost did turn myself into the hospital, but just the thought of going through this training again was enough to keep me going. It was enough to drive me crazy. The training itself was physical, but I could do it. The discipline was strict, but I could take it. However, the in-betweens, the harassment, the belittlement, the pettiness, the beratings, the corporal punishment, the brainwashing, and the bullshit—the plain, unadulterated bullshit that accompanied every orientated speech would be most difficult to repeat without killing some son of a bitch. So I decided to keep going as long as I possibly could.

Everyone at this time was giving me advice on how to cure my foot. It was do this or do that, and then take this and take that. I did appreciate my friends' concern; it was so encouraging, comforting, and heartwarming. It kept me going for weeks.

The following day we had a repeat performance under the hot sun, and fewer than ten men survived Horton's death marches, as they were now called. This last time I came pretty close to passing out. I could see the black sunspots before my eyes, the flashes of heat that surround your head, the dizziness that accompanies these symptoms. As I stumbled onward, I prayed to St. Anthony for strength, sometimes aloud, and he always heard my prayer. His statue was always in my pocket above my heart. I placed a lot of trust on that saint, and he never failed me. It was most comforting to know that you had a friend upstairs.

That night I really limped into the barracks and flopped on my sack, thanking God it was Saturday night and there would be no marching in the morning. Tomorrow we were getting our first layoff in five weeks. It wasn't exactly a day off, but there would be no training. Monday we were shooting small arms on the pistol range and Tuesday we were leaving this area for the rifle range. We would be there for a month, and then out of this godforsaken land and home for ten whole days. Ten days to sleep, ten days to eat, and ten days to what? Just thinking about it brought goose pimples to my skin. Just thinking about it elated me and raised my morale a hundred percent.

We had completed five full weeks of training, and it was now the middle of July. Everything was moving right along. If only my foot would heal, that would be asking too much. If only it didn't get any worse. That's it; if only it didn't get any worse.

Bob Humpfrey, the Southerner from Georgia, came over to my sack. He introduced himself and asked if he could take a look at my foot. He said, in his thick Southern drawl, that I had a full-blown infection and that it was spreading rapidly and could turn into blood poisoning if it were neglected. He advised me to go to sick bay (hospital). I looked at him in a sort of a wise-ass way and blurted out, "No shit, is that what you think it is? Well, I don't take any Southerner's word on anything, so screw! Don't waste your breath on me." He looked at me in surprise and I could see he was taken aback by my remark. This was my first association with Humpfrey. Anyone who was from the South was on my shit list. I wanted nothing to do with Southerners. Furthermore, I was not a person to hide my feelings, and even though I obeyed every order and every command, one would have to be half blind not to see the contempt I had for Southerners—all Southerners.

Humpfrey had become the favorite boy of the platoon. He and Moore were the only Southerners in our outfit, and Horton, the sergeant, only spoke to Humpfrey. Mo said Humpfrey's daddy had money and every Monday there was a check for the sergeant. Perhaps, but you couldn't prove it by me. He may have come from Okefenokee country, but he was no backwoodsman.

The next morning he sat at our chow table without even being asked. "Look," he said, "I have a plan about your foot, man. I think I can help you. Let me try. I just want to be friendly." To get rid of him, I agreed to see him in the barracks.

When I returned from the mess hall, the pain in the ass was sitting on my bunk waiting for me. I couldn't believe it. "Well," he cried, "hi, buddy, been waiting for you. I got all the gear. Let's git started." I saw the wash pail and four bottles of Clorox and No Worry washing fluid, and then I started to laugh. "Where's the snake oil? What the hell is this, an Okefenokee cure-all?" He didn't say anything but proceeded to empty all the bottles into the pail. The aroma of Clorox fumes was terrible. "Take off your sock," he screamed. "Let's git started." Then he looked at my messy sores. There were a million of them, so it seemed, and they were up to my leg. Each sore was oozing pus. It was disgusting. "God!" he said. "What a mess." As I put my foot in the washing fluid, wow! Did it sting! Did it burn! Did it hurt! It just brought tears to your eyes.

I soaked my foot in that water pail for two consecutive hours. Humpfrey checked on it periodically. He reminded me of a cook who had a roast beef in the oven. He would examine the foot closely and then say, "Leave it in a little while longer." Finally, after two hours had passed, he came over and authoritatively said, in his slow Southern drawl, "Lay down a towel, boy. Now take your foot out of that bucket. Put your foot on that towel and don't touch it. Let that stuff dry as is." Then with a smile, "How does it feel, boy?"

I replied, "It burns and it hurts." Every bit of skin was burned off my leg and foot. It looked raw.

"Yeah, man!" Humpfrey said. "It's cooked all right." Then he started to give advice. "Now look, for the next two hours, don't even move. The boys will carry you out in the shade, and you just let the good old air get at it. It's going to be all right. I'm going down to the hospital now and get some light bandage."

"Hell!" I exclaimed. "I don't want you to get into any trouble over me."

"Don't you worry about it, fella," he replied. "I'm not gitting into any trouble. I already done got permission from Sergeant Horton to git to the hospital. I'll be back in a spell," and he left.

The hospital was located a good four miles from our barracks. My friends Corr, Pierce, Setzer, and Panos carried me outside, and I sat on a box with my foot high in the air.

Everybody and anybody from everywhere came over to look at my foot. They were all sympathetic but some in a crude sort of way. Some just looked at it and left. Others made a face and left. Some said, "God," and left. Some fellows said it looked like the crud—whatever crud looks like. Others said it looked like the *mange*, and some thought the foot was turning blue. One said matter-of-factly that he saw better-looking feet amputated.

"Doc" Humpfrey returned from the hospital with some salve and rolls of bandages. My friends carried me back to my sack, and Humpfrey went to work. He spread a little salve on my shinbone and ankle, but applied nothing to my feet, not even powder. Then he started applying the bandage, before an audience of forty boots. He proceeded to tie up my foot into a neat little package. Everyone commented he sure did act like a doctor, and that he should have been a corpsman. He advised me to stay off my feet until tomorrow morning. The foot was still very sore and painful, and Doc Humpfrey insisted I take a couple of pills. I assumed he picked them up at the hospital, but what they were, I'll never know. I fell asleep in a matter of minutes. It was around six o'clock in the evening, and I never woke up till they were playing "Reveille."

It was one big beautiful dream, and I woke up like a person who had slept for a week. I felt so terrific, and the pain in my foot had abated to such an extent that I felt like jumping on the floor. Humpfrey was over before I was fully dressed. "How's it going, fella?" he asked.

"Great, just great," I replied. I extended my hand and he accepted it. "Thanks ... thanks for everything. You're quite a guy."

He just looked at me and smiled. "I don't know how you stood that pain for so many weeks. You're quite a guy yourself. See you later," and he took off.

I put two pairs of socks on my foot and although it was sore, it was nothing like it was before the Clorox treatment. Marching to chow was a test and it held up good.

This morning our platoon was shooting small arms for record, and Sergeant Horton was as tense as a cat on a hot tin roof. He was pacing up and down that barracks floor like a caged panther.

Whenever a platoon does anything for recognition or there is competition between platoons, then the drill instructor and his assistant have friendly and not-so-friendly bets between or among platoon leaders. That is one of the reasons the boots are pushed to such an extent. The drill instructor wants perfection in his lash-up. He demands it and he gets it. All men are expendable in time of war, and this is war. The bets between platoon leaders could run as high as a thousand dollars, or as much as you're willing to bet. No matter what the price, somebody will cover it. Humpfrey, the Southerner, who came about as close as anyone to knowing Sergeant Horton and Corporal Howard, informed us that the sergeant and corporal had bet over a thousand dollars on us to win the pistol match and that we would be in competition with a least five platoons. Winners reap and losers weep; so the slogan goes. Well, I could never see Sergeant Horton weeping, so if we didn't win, we were in for a lot of hell.

We were on the pistol range by 0700 (navy time) and excitement was running high. The men shot in small groups of six or more. It was all offhand shooting, and to be a good pistol shot, you had to know how to apply correctly the four points in shooting: (1) method of holding the pistol, (2) position, (3) trigger squeeze, and (4) alignment of sights. You face your body left (or nearly so) from the line of aim. Your feet are placed twelve to eighteen inches apart, and your head is erect with body perfectly balanced. Your left hand may be held in three positions: (1) on the left hip, (2) thumb in left pocket, or (3) hanging naturally by the side. I was taught with my left hand on hip, and it was natural and comfortable this way. You always use your shoulder to direct the pistol on the target, never your elbow or wrist, because the arm will not be steady. This causes quick and erratic movement of the pistol, and results in trembling and jerking the trigger. The trigger squeeze is the same as with the rifle, and while aiming and firing, you hold your breath. Your sights are aligned this way: the top of the front sight is level with and in the center of the notch of the rear sight. "We are now ready to proceed with the pistol exercise. It will consist of slow fire and rapid fire at fifteen- and twenty-five-yard range. The time limit for shooting five shots in rapid fire is eleven seconds. At twenty-five yards in quick fire, the target is exposed three seconds for each shot and then turned away for two seconds. Then you bring your pistol into position just as the target is exposed and fire again." All platoons were participating, and the shooting coaches were recording the scores.

After we had all participated in shooting at the bull's-eye and silhouette targets at the fifteen-yard range, we then moved to the twenty-five-yard range. Each man would shoot at least fifty times.

After one hour of competition, we moved into the last position: quick fire at twenty-five-yard range, silhouette targets. Tension was mounting as each shot rang out. Sergeant Horton was there rooting for his platoon and spurred each man on as he approached the firing line. Everyone in our platoon seemed to be doing well, and the competition was now down to only two outfits—and ours, Sergeant Horton's was one of them.

Finally, the competition narrowed down to only two of us. I was nervous, restless, and fidgety and paced up and down the line. Right before I was to shoot, the sergeant approached me. He grabbed me by the arm. "Summers," he said, "it's all up to you, boy! Don't let us down. You can do it, boy! Just squeeze them off. Take your time, just squeeze them off. Easy does it." I didn't say a word, but with a somber, straight face, I looked directly into his squinty green eyes. His face, now tense, reflected his concern like pondering the outcome, and his teeth were biting down on his lower lip. This man wanted to win bad—very bad. This man was pleading with me to win. This was the closest I'd ever seen him come to being human. This was the closest I'd ever seen him talk civilly to a person. I thought in a few minutes Sergeant Horton would be richer by thousands or—and I couldn't say the word, but I knew either way he would always remember this moment. He would never forget, and he would never forgive. He was that kind of a man. The pressure was immense.

I approached the firing line and loaded my pistol. With my left hand entrenched on my hip, I waited for the target to appear. The target appeared. Slowly I raised my weapon and fired. Again and again as that target appeared, I fired. Reloading, I continued to fire at those silhouette targets as they came up and disappeared. And then it was all over. I did my best, and I was oblivious as to what was taking place. As I turned around and headed back toward the rest area, Sergeant Horton was there to greet me. His green eyes were dancing with joy, and the rugged features of his face were shining with smiles. He was happy. "Good shooting, boy!" he exclaimed. "Good shooting! You did it. You didn't miss once. Beautiful, beautiful, man! You did it. You made it, boy!" And he then took off, probably to collect his money. The men didn't say too much and you didn't expect them to. In predicaments like this, especially concerning the DI, it's better not to say too much, for few of us knew what was going on, and the majority of us didn't care. In your own mind, there was peace and in your heart there was joy. Confidence just surged through your veins. You had accomplished something. You were a marine—a good marine—you knew it, and it made you feel proud. Proud to be an American.

That night in our barracks there was joy and, for the first time, men were talking about their exploits in everything from football to girls. Within a matter of minutes, all hell broke loose, from a peaceful existence to bedlam.

Sergeant Horton had come back to the barracks. Scuttlebutt rumors had it that the sergeant was taking a seventy-two-hour leave, and that he would rejoin our platoon on the rifle range. We were scheduled to leave in the morning. Sergeant Horton entered our barracks through the front door, and no one had seen him enter. He didn't waste any time doing what he came to do. Corporal Howard accompanied him as he hustled through the barracks. Before anyone recognized him, the action was already starting. I saw Corporal Howard lie on a bottom sack and with his two feet swinging in the air, he kicked upward. The soles of his two feet met the spring and the mattress with such force that Alfonso Moore, who was lying on his back, flew into the air in a horizontal position. Then Sergeant Horton, who was standing on the side of the iron bed, pushed him while he was in midair like a basketball assist, propelling him against the other bed. He fell downward toward the wooden floor and landed in a heap. Quickly, Corporal Howard grabbed him by his neck and pulled him upright in a hurry. Once Moore was on his feet, Sergeant Horton took over. He raged and he snarled, "Why, you goddamn long drink of piss. You thought I was kidding when I said don't sell any pogey-bait [candy] to my platoon. Well, shit-for-brains, I'm gonna show you, boy!" With that he took out his knife, and the blade was flashing in his hands. "You're going to get a full military funeral, boy, and it won't cost you one cent, not one goddamn penny." He then took the knife and in one swift motion, I saw him plunge that knife into Moore's body. So did the rest of the platoon. The silence was deafening.

Moore's mouth opened wide, and his eyes seem to pop in his head. We waited for him to fall, but he never fell. Instead, his three money belts fell to the floor. The sergeant had cut them right off his person without drawing a drop of blood. It was funny, but we knew better than to even smile. "Git your gear, Private Moore. You're out of my platoon, and I'm putting you in for a court-martial. I'm charging you with willful disobedience, insubordination. I'm hoping you get a bad conduct discharge. And I'm telling the rest of you now, anyone disobeying my orders gets the same punishment as Moore. I'll make you wish that you never saw the corps. The three men I caught tonight will ride the kitchen range for a week. Beginning tonight, they will spend six hours in the galley." With that remark, they took off for the sergeant's quarters. We knew for sure that Alfonso Moore would be beaten to a pulp once he entered the sergeant's office. The rest of the evening was quiet.

CHAPTER XI

Right after chow the following morning, we left for the rifle range. In a few weeks, when we returned, our training would be over and we would be leaving on a ten-day furlough. That thought spurred you on.

The rifle range area was a rather pleasant place compared to the drilling sites. It was almost like a resort area. We were very close to the water, and sea breezes were always blowing across the range. During the day, the hot sun beat down unmercifully on the flat terrain. It baked the land like an infrared lamp, and as the air stirred from the breeze coming from the sea, you could actually feel the hot masses of heat surging through your body.

The living quarters on the rifle range were similar to the barracks at the other end of the island. They were long wooden structures, nothing elaborate, with just plain cutouts for windows, and with no glass or screening in them. The large entrances on both sides of the building were without doors. It was just as plain inside, nothing fancy. You had a deck to walk on, a roof to protect you from the elements, and a bed to sleep on. That was it; that completed the scene. Five weeks ago, I turned my nose up at this kind of a setup, and then it was awful. Now it was beautiful, which proves again that happiness is a state of being. Indoctrination was a wonderful thing. Our dispositions were also changing. We had absorbed so much punishment in the last five weeks, both physical and mental, that now we knew that anything they dished out, we could take. We were that conditioned.

The first thing they changed at the range was reveille. We hit the decks at 3:00 in the morning—the middle of the night. Chow in the morning was at 3:30 a.m. and by 4:30 we were on the road, marching to the rifle range. We marched in the streets, and the sound of footsteps hitting the pavement, all in unison, in the darkness of night was music to Sergeant Horton's ears. You could feel it, for even in the blackness, the musical sound of his cadence rent the night air like a curtain, so loud and so clear that the syllables sounded like prayers. In the distance you could also hear the other platoons marching to the cadence of their drill instructors, but Sergeant Horton's cadence had a very special sound, sort of a flare combined with a rhythm that was different from all the rest, and it sure sounded the best.

Once on the rifle range, we were instructed to make sure the bolt on our rifle was open at all times when we were off the firing line. Safety was stressed at all times, so much so that it became boring to listen to, but it was a necessary precaution. With weapons there is never any horseplay; it's all business. Your rifle is your calling card. You never pointed it at anyone unless you intended to kill that person. That statement was instilled in us through indoctrination.

The first thing we were issued on the range was a shooting jacket. This was a padded coat worn when shooting the rifle to prevent shoulders and elbows from becoming sore. Soreness can cause shooters to become gun-shy and flinch. When a man flinches, then he is expecting the explosion and the recoil. He shoves his shoulder forward, pulls (instead of squeezing) the trigger, shuts his eyes, and misses the bull's-eye or target. A shooting jacket is generally one or two sizes too big to allow for necessary freedom of movement.

There were smudge pots located behind the firing lines, and you blackened your sights to prevent reflection of light from the sights. You drew your live ammo and approached the firing line. The sun was starting to rise, and it was approximately 0700 navy time.

The rifle range was a well-planned, beautiful grassy area. Facing out, poking into the sea, the grassy mounds designated the different firing ranges. They stood out like statues, developing in your mind a picture of complete peacefulness and serenity. The blue sky and the bright sun just added to the picture. Once the firing commenced, the noise alone changed the place into a frightening aspect. You knew this was a factory, a place where you learned how to kill.

We heard, "Everyone will shoot right-handed; there will be no exceptions to the rules. The positions you will shoot will be standing offhand, kneeling position, sitting position, and prone position. The distances will be two hundred yards, three hundred yards, and five hundred yards. The weeks of studying your rifle will now be applied. Everything you have learned about your rifle will be shown to you by professionals. It will be interesting, educational, and—believe it or not—fun." Shooting was fun. However, they forced certain positions on you, and you had to do it their way. At times it wasn't easy. To me, the kneeling was the most difficult to master. In a kneeling position, you sit on your right foot or your right heel. They insisted we sit on our right foot. I had an old football injury on my right leg at the kneecap. It was fine as long as I didn't bend my knee too long. Telling the marines about it was the wrong thing. Such thing wrong thing! To make sure that my leg was tucked under correctly, one marine sat on my shoulders and another marine stood on my right leg. The pain was terrific, but they joked how that in a half-hour the leg would go to sleep and I wouldn't feel anything. After half an hour, the leg was asleep, but it was hurting like hell. To get them off my back, I told them it was okay, and I learned to shoot that way. Private Monahan had trouble with his back, and in a prone position it hurt. Two marines stood on his back for an hour to prove it didn't hurt. They worked over half of our platoon, and some of the men had tears in their eyes from being stepped on by these asshole marine coaches.

After the first week of training on the range, any boot could get into any position, anywhere, anytime, and hit a bull's-eye nine times out of ten. We learned our lessons the hard way, but the right way. Everything was so well-planned and organized at the rifle range that you automatically did things instinctively. We learned the direction and force of wind on shooting and applied the windage rule. We learned the horizontal clock system to designate the direction of the wind and the effect of light on shooting. We also learned to describe the location of hits on a target—it was called the vertical clock system. We also learned how to zero a rifle. The zero of a rifle is the point at which the rear sight must be set, both for elevation and windage, to hit the center of the bull's-eye when there is no wind and other conditions are normal.

Special ordinance men looked over your rifle periodically while on the range. They made necessary adjustments and replaced worn-out parts. The rifle that we were shooting with was a United States rifle, caliber .30, model 1903. The popular name of this service rifle is called a Springfield rifle. It is a breech-loading, magazine-fed, bolt-operated shoulder weapon. The weight of the rifle is 8.69 pounds. The magazine will hold five cartridges, and the average marine can fire ten aimed shots per minute. Its most effective ranges are up to six hundred yards. At six hundred yards, it can still penetrate a quarter-inch steel plate. It is the most effective individual infantry weapon.

When we weren't shooting, we were working the pits. I can't say it was the most enjoyable place to spend a summer afternoon, but it was interesting and educational. This is where all the action was located and recorded. The Butts reminded me of a World War I trench. Wooden frames outlined the structure and sandbags were stacked inside those frames. Row upon row of sandbags fifteen to twenty feet high outlined that structure. At each end of the line, men were operating the telephones. There was always direct communication between the Butts and the firing line. Everything between the two lines was synchronized.

The targets lined up like soldiers, all in a row. Perhaps there were thirty targets, maybe more, and each target was manned by three or four men. The targets fitted into wooden frames, and the wooden frames were connected to pulleys. You could raise or lower them or half-mast them, depending upon the coaches' commands.

The NCOs in charge of the Butts continually walked up and down the line. They explained that all targets are run up or down simultaneously. When the bell rang the first time, you ran them up and when it rang again, you pulled them down. Then the Butt coaches would holler, "Mark those targets," and you would look for the bullet holes. If it was a bull's-eye you waved a white flag for five points, and a black flag for four points. A checkered flag indicated three points and a half-black and half-white meant two points. If you couldn't find any hits, then you knew he missed the target entirely, and you waved a red flag. The red flag was fondly called "Maggie's drawers." After marking your target, you then patched up the holes. Glue, brushes, and patches were right in the target section, and once that job was completed, you half-masted your target to await the next command. No one was allowed to leave the Butts until the order "cease-fire" was given. The last group to work the Butts had to police the area. Everything was neatly put away until the next working day.

Living on the rifle range wasn't all that bad. The chow even tasted better here, or perhaps we were getting use to it. Reveille was at 5:00 a.m., and we fell out for roll call immediately, and then we ran a full mile and went in the barracks, made up the sacks, and went to chow. Every minute of your working day was planned until it became routine.

Our first Sunday at the rifle range they took us to the pool, and for three or four hours we enjoyed swimming. You had to take precautions against getting sunburned. If you had to report to sick bay for sunburn, you left yourself open for a court-martial, so you made sure you covered up in that hot sun.

The following Sunday they asked us if we would like to see a movie show. Betty Grable was the main attraction, and every hand was raised. We all wanted to go. It was the week before we were to shoot for record, and the weather was extremely hot and humid.

Sergeant Horton marched us to the theater, and we were all dressed in khaki uniforms, including scarves (ties). We wore our overseas caps and as a group, we did look sharp—real sharp—and we were proud. It showed in our walk and our actions. Our training had paid off.

We entered the movie theater in orderly fashion. Marching down the aisles, we filled the orchestra seats quickly. It was a small theater that held 250 people comfortably, but tonight it was packed to capacity with well over 300 people. The excitement of seeing a Betty Grable picture ran high, and the movie started exactly at 1930 navy time (7:30 p.m.). We screamed when the lights dimmed, and we screeched when the Bugs Bunny cartoon appeared. The Pathe News brought rousing cheers as moving pictures of our servicemen in action in the war zones appeared on the screen. Then the main feature started, and Betty Grable's picture on the screen brought down the house. These marines were hungry-happy, they were starved for this kind of entertainment, and they were a most appreciative audience.

Once the main movie started, most of us noticed it was becoming uncomfortably warm in the theater, and then we realized why. Every door was closed tight and every window was secured. These rotten, sadistic bastards had turned on the heat. In no time at all, the theater felt like a hot oven. It was like a steam room; you could hardly breathe. The men became disorderly and wanted to leave the hot building.

Then the lights came on and a marine officer with a Southern drawl spoke from the stage. His speech was short and to the point. "Y'all wanted to see a movie, and y'all are seeing a movie. Now shut yo goddamn mouths and look at yo movie." The lights went out.

Screams and jeers greeted the officer's remarks, followed by profanity—lots of it. The lights came back on. All was quiet. The officer spoke again. "Make up yo mind … heah me! Y'all is staying heah till this heah movie is over. Any more catcalls, and y'all will stay and see it over agin. Heah me?" The lights went out again and the movie continued playing, but no one under these conditions could watch it, even with Betty Grable, the number one pinup girl, as the main attraction. We were slowly being cooked. Our khaki shirts, pants, and socks were soaking wet. It was terrible, and the heat was unbearable. Men passed out from the heat, but we were instructed to leave them alone. The NCO screamed to let them lie there. "They'll be all right. If they can't take it, they shouldn't be here." In all the hours we spent there, we didn't grow accustomed to the heat. You remained as quiet as possible and accepted it. I prayed to St. Anthony and offered this heat up as penance for the poor souls in purgatory.

At 10:50 p.m., when all the souls were released from purgatory, they said we could leave. We left the theater, dripping wet, but again in orderly fashion, knowing for sure that a little more of our mind had been indoctrinated. No one said a word. Automatically, we fell into two ranks. We covered down. Sergeant Horton screamed, "Attention! Right face—forward, march. Aaaa wan … Aaaa reap … a two fo you lept two, three, four. Your leaf … yo left high loaf," and we proceeded to march to our barracks. You couldn't help thinking. It was one of those nights that confused you. Perhaps we don't know the real enemy.

Well, one consolation: one more week and we would be leaving this place. Yes! Leaving Parris Island forever.

N. M. C. 1150—A&I
(Revised 1942)

United States Marine Corps

Serial No. ___415932___

Unit ___Quartermaster___

___School.___

Headquarters, School Battalion, Training
Center, Fleet Marine Force, Marine Barracks,
New River, North Carolina.

___13 November, 1942.___

___HENRY A. SOMMERELL___

by the direction of the Commandant of the Marine Corps, is hereby appointed a

___CORPORAL___

in the UNITED STATES MARINE CORPS ___RESERVE___, and he is therefore carefully and diligently to discharge the duties of that position by doing and performing all manner of things thereunto belonging. I do strictly charge and require all Noncommissioned Officers and others under his command to be obedient to his orders, and he is to observe and follow such orders and directions from time to time as he shall receive from his Commanding Officer or other superior officers set over him, according to the rules and discipline of the Navy. To rank from 13 November, 1942.

Type ___"TEMPORARY"___
(SHIP'S, PERMANENT)

Branch ___(SPECIAL) (CLERICAL) "ON DUTY"___
(LINE, AVIATION, COMMUNICATION)

Authority ___Bat Instr No. 181, dated 13nov42___
(MARINE CORPS MANUAL (IR C. M. C. LTR. (DATE))

R. M. MONTAGUE,
___Colonel___, U. S. M. C.,

No. ___-32-___
LOWEST NUMBER OF SAME
DATE TAKEN RANK

Commanding ___School Battalion.___

(ORIGINAL)

★ GPO 16—26276-2

CHAPTER XII

Monday and Tuesday were rough training days. We were practicing shooting continually, and we were running the bayonet course too. Monday we ran the bayonet course for record, and our platoon did very well as a group.

The bayonet course was a long run, over two hundred yards long. There were obstacles all along the run and while you were running, you had to scream at your potential enemy. You parry right and you parry left, and then you stick your bayonet into your target, kick the body with your feet, and pull out the bayonet and continue to the next figure. Running at full steam, you slash your weapon in an upward thrust like an uppercut in the boxing ring, and the plate of your rifle smashes the jaw of your make-believe enemy, knocking him backward. You thrust your bayonet into his stomach and again you kick your foot into his belly or groin and pull out your bayonet, taking off at high speed. Screaming at the top of your lungs, you encounter your next obstacle, and so on down the course. At the finish line, there is a silhouette target and on a full run you hit the deck, making sure your rifle stock absorbs all the shock after landing. From a prone position, you fire five shots in rapid fire into that silhouette target.

I was an expert in bayonet fighting, and Sergeant Horton paid me a tribute by saying I did a commendable job. He observed every man in his platoon through his field glasses, and he never missed a trick. His concern with his troops was amazing. When you finished the run, he was there to greet you. He never pulled any punches, and he never left you hanging. His comments were favorable or unfavorable. Sergeant Horton wasn't the least concerned about your feelings. He was a very outspoken man, and on more than one occasion he would tell some boots that they should have joined the navy or the Boy Scouts; they would never make marines.

On Tuesday we finished working the obstacle course, hand-to-hand training, and hand-grenade training. Now the only thing left on our schedule was shooting the rifle. Wednesday was preliminary target day and everything was the same as record day, except the averages were not being recorded.

The morning of preliminary shooting day arrived, and it was a most beautiful day. The weather was calm and rather cool, and hardly any wind was blowing. Furthermore, it would all be over by noontime, and no afternoon hot sun to contend with. Normally, if you made a good score today, then you could rest assure your score would be about the same or very close to it on record day.

Everything went along perfectly and systematically and before very long it was all over. Our platoon had shot well as a group; over 90 percent had qualified. Sergeant Horton was very pleased with the outcome. He wore a smirk on his face, a self-assured look that proclaimed to the world, "I have a good team, a real good team … a real good team."

In this platoon, no one man stood out. We were a close-knit group of men. After a month of training, every man was accepted as an individual. Even the goofballs were accepted. We came to feel sorry for the unfortunates. We realized how difficult life was here, and we accepted other people's problems as our own. In the evening, you saw men helping others, listening to their bitches, hearing their lessons, showing men what they're doing wrong. But being kind was the most important thing. Kindness led to acceptance, and being accepted into a group meant that you had friends—and friendship in a place like this made life that much easier.

Our part of the barracks had become the living room of the platoon. Men congregated here, all problems were discussed here, and sound advice was freely given by knowledgeable recruits. Card games were played here every night. All the action originated between these four sacks. The two youngest marines in our outfit were always present. Private Fiber from Schenectady, New York, was coming out of his shell. I amazed him with my stamina, surprised him with my agility, and dazzled him with how fast I could throw a punch. Three weeks earlier, I had defended him against a group of marines. No one challenged me, and since then they had left him alone. He considered me a friend, and as time passed on, he was accepted.

Private Gallenhurst spent many hours around our bunk. He was a big boy and strong as a bull. His nickname was "Stash," and Joe Setzer took him under his wing. He befriended him in many ways, showing him how to shoot, how to bat, and telling him he could be another Lou Gehrig. He tried to build up his ego, but today everything had collapsed. Stash shot 188 on the rifle range, and he didn't qualify; neither did Harold Fiber. They both felt bad. God! How they wanted to belong. We told them tomorrow they would shoot real good—you watch; everything's going to be real good. It made them happy, talking this way. It gave them faith. They always had hope.

All my friends, including myself, did very well. Joe Setzer shot the highest, 233 out of a possible 250. Corr was second at 230, followed by Pierce at 228, and Panos at 225. Pinto and I both shot 218; Humpfrey shot 214. These scores were excellent, from expert to sharpshooter. However, the majority of the men shot marksman. Pvt. Pat Monahan shot a low 178, and he was feeling dejected. We tried building up his spirits too.

Corporal Howard came into the barracks, and he gave us a quiz on our rifle. Private Setzer and Forrest Corr gave a unique demonstration of assembling their dismantled rifles blindfolded. Before the evening was over, most of us had accomplished this same feat. There was no doubt about it, we knew our weapon. We were ready for the big day.

The morning we shot for record, the excitement and pressure started at the crack of dawn with the sound of reveille. It started slowly at first, and then continually built up until we hit the rifle range. Here we moved into high gear and stayed there the rest of the day.

We had proved to our coaches and drill instructors that we could all shoot a rifle. Now we had to prove to everyone that we were qualified to shoot that rifle. Preliminary day was over. The fact that you shot expert didn't count. It never went into the books. This was the one day they recorded—this was the one for the records. This was it.

To qualify on the rifle, one had to shoot a score of 196 points out of a possible 250. Considering that the army qualified at 166 points, this was no mean feat. All of us were confident, all of us were alert. We were shooting at two hundred yards, three hundred yards, and five hundred yards, slow fire and rapid fire, with bull's-eye and silhouette targets.

When we arrived at the rifle range at 4:30 in the morning, it was still pitch-black, and there was a sort of a mist in the air. When we moved up to the two-hundred-yard line, the mist had turned into a drizzle of rain. A stiff wind was blowing in from the sea, thus splashing your face with tiny little raindrops. You bundled up in your shooting jacket. It felt good, and prevented the water from trickling down your neck. At the moment, despite the wind and the rain, you were quite comfortable. Normally, the weather at this time of the year is hot and humid. The forecast had called for a hot, calm day. However, Parris Island, situated on the water, was subject to unpredictable storms. Warnings were posted every day to alert small craft; sea squalls and tornadoes were not uncommon here.

The wind velocity does not affect your weapon at two hundred or three hundred yards, but at five hundred yards, the wind could prove a factor. Because of the adverse weather conditions, we commenced shooting at daybreak. The weather would not cancel our shooting match, for a postponement would mean an extra day of training, which would affect the schedules of other platoons. Therefore, the brass couldn't care less how the weather would affect us and our shooting. Even if it was snowing, it would be up to us to adjust. The most famous word in the Marine Corps is "improvise," and that's what we did. We adjusted our windage accordingly, and Sergeant Horton gave us a brief pep talk. Looking very determined, and not the least concerned about the weather, he stated matter-of-factly, "You men know how to shoot. Don't worry about the rain." Then he added, to build up our ego, "The elements won't have any effect upon your score. Good luck." Then, scanning his troops with his hawklike eyes, he left, but I'm sure he was thinking of the thousand dollars that was riding on his platoon.

We stood on the firing line, two hundred yards offhand shooting. The coach's deep voice bellowed over the bullhorn, "Ready on the right … ready on the left. Load and lock. Unlock." The targets came up from the Butts. "Commence firing," and record day was now in progress. It sounded like the Fourth of July.

The two-hundred- and three-hundred-yard lines caused us very little or no trouble at all. My rapid fire in all positions was excellent, and my slow-fire aim was good. The wind didn't seem to bother us at all, but the water trickling down your face took away from your concentration on slow fire. And when we hit the five-hundred-yard line, things started to go bad for me and some of my friends. There were six of us shooting on the far outside target nearest to the sea. Private Clyde Simmons shot first, and we watched intensely as he squeezed the trigger again and again. Ten times he shot in the prone position. Prone shooting is a natural position and the most comfortable position. It's the easiest shooting position and also the steadiest to handle your rifle. However, when they totaled Private Simmons's score, he had missed the target completely four times, and not one of his shots landed in the bull's-eye. He couldn't believe it, and neither could we. The next man to shoot was Private Pinto, who was an excellent shot. He too had a poor performance and missed the target completely two times. All six of us men ended up with very poor scores on the five hundred slow-fire target.

Sergeant Horton couldn't believe it. His face was red, his eyes glared, and his lips twitched. He seemed to be arguing with the coach as if putting the blame on him. The coach did set each of our sights, and he did check out our windage. Whether he miscalculated at such a crucial time or whether it was the bad weather, we will never know. The damage was done, and the books were closed.

I checked and rechecked my score. I shot 195 and Pinto shot 194. Fifteen of us didn't qualify. This was a disaster.

Despite our bad shooting, there were some bright spots. Seven out of the ten men who didn't qualify on preliminary day qualified today. Private Monahan, who never shot more than 180 at any time during practice, shot 197 today and qualified. He was happy as a lark. However, the surprise of the day was the two young kids, Private Fiber and Private Gallenhurst. These men had been the fall guys of the platoon ever since we began training. They were the goats, never the heroes. Few kind words ever came their way, and they felt rejected, but today everything changed. Today, on this unbelievable field, under the most adverse weather conditions, they shot expert. Sergeant Horton stood in front of our platoon and gave out the shooting scores, and then he called the two young men out of the ranks. "I want to congratulate these two men for their shooting. They shot the highest scores in our platoon, and under the worst conditions this island has had in the last six months. Private Gallenhurst's score was an incredible 240 out of a possible 250, and Private Fiber shot 236 out of a possible 250 to take second place." The sergeant smiled, something we didn't think he was capable of, and he continued, "I can't call them shitheads anymore. They're men—real men. They're United States Marines." Then, extending his hand, he congratulated them. Their eyes filled with water. This was the man who had caused them so much grief and anguish. This was the man who berated them, and the man who humiliated them. He was now extending his hand in friendship. Yes! There were tears. They had come a long way.

Then, without warning and without being dismissed, the men broke ranks, and racing toward the young men, they hoisted them on their shoulders and carried them into the barracks. They were elated and filled with emotion and were laughing and crying at the same time. Looking back in retrospect, it seemed like only yesterday that they were being carried to the showers, beaten and humiliated. "Time heals everything."

"Time heals everything." Those famous last words played over and over again in my mind. I was so disappointed for not qualifying that I couldn't think clearly. It bothered me so that I didn't go to chow that night. It gnawed at me. I had nothing to talk about. It ate at me. I had nothing to cheer about and nothing to celebrate. My friends kept their distance. They said nothing except they were sorry. All of them had qualified and were whooping it up. They were happy and they showed it, asking me to join them. I made excuses. I couldn't; I just couldn't.

Private Humpfrey came over, discreetly asking about my foot. In four weeks, it had healed up miraculously. I had a new layer of skin, and it looked beautiful. He continued his conversation in his slow Southern drawl, "Boy! Y'all have a lot to be thankful for. Forget about that range. Snap out of yo shit, man." I told him I couldn't. "Man," he continued, "I'd love to give you my 215 score, if you would give me your guts, your stamina, your expertise on the pistol, on the bayonet, your hand-to-hand combat physical record." I laughed a sickly laugh. "I mean it, boy. I really mean it. You have a lot going for you." I dismissed him by saying I would see him in a little while, and I slowly walked away.

At my bunk I sat there thinking, just thinking what might have been. I decided to write a letter to my Ma. I had to get this off my chest, and there was no better person to tell than my Ma. I got out my equipment and started to write immediately.

Dear Ma,

I don't know where to begin this letter, for I find it most difficult to write. Today was qualifying day with the rifle, and I missed qualifying by one point. I wanted so badly to make a good score, but I failed. Yes, I failed, and I feel rejected. True, I can blame it on the weather (it rained continually). True, I can blame it on the coach for goofing on the windage. But no, Ma. I can only blame myself. I did the shooting, and I did not shoot my potential. Perhaps I didn't try hard enough. No, I tried ... I tried my best, and it wasn't good enough. At Parris Island, you get no second chance. Inwardly, I feel awful.

Ma, no matter how bad I feel, when I talk things over with you, I do feel better. Say a prayer that this feeling passes quickly. I'll be coming home in about a week. Hoping everything at home is fine. "Thank God for mothers."

Your loving son, Henry

The time was 2000 hours navy time (8:00 p.m.). I lay in my sack, thinking, thinking all the time, pondering the future and rehashing the past. *This last week*, I thought, *has been a bitch, a real bitch.* Again I thought, *next week I'm going home.* Yes! For ten whole days, I'll be home. I had thirty-five dollars in my possession. Not much, but the fare would only cost ten dollars. Servicemen traveling on the railroad were allowed half fare, thank God; and if I could get a ride to North Carolina, it would only be eight dollars. I was figuring out my finances and seeing how I could stretch them. Well, everyone in my family would be good for five. Yeah! I'd make it, but my money still was limited.

Then I heard someone say, "Attention!" and I jumped off my sack onto the wooden deck. "As you were," retorted Sergeant Horton. "Men, gather round heah! I have something to tell you." He began, "Today on the range, some of you fared better than others. It wasn't the best shooting weather, but then I've seen worse. I'm not here to make any alibis, but I do have good news for a few of you. The rifle coaches have reviewed the targets in the Butts, and the following men have picked up a few extra points."

My face lightened up, my mind activated, and my whole being came alive. *God,* I prayed. *Please, God,* I said. *Dear God,* I pleaded. *Let me pick up one lousy point.* Then, *Dear God, please God,* over and over again I prayed.

"Private Corr, they found three points in the Butts. Your score is now 216. You're now a sharpshooter. Private Pierce, two points. Your score is now 210. Private Pinto, three points brings you to 197." A rousing cheer went up. He had now qualified as did three others.

Down the list he went, and my very life seemed to hang on his every word. "Summers, two points. You qualify with 197, marksman. Jones, 202, marksman. And that's it. I know some of you men tried so hard and failed, others didn't try hard enough, but as a platoon, your average was good." Then he added, "The best average for the day." He smiled. We roared approval. We knew he won the money pool. He then said, "Carry on," and left the squad room.

Bob Humpfrey was the first one to congratulate me. Running over with a shit-eating grin on his face, he cried, "See, boy! All that fuss and fuming over nothing." All I could do was smile. My head was in the clouds. All my friends shook my hand. Everything was fine again. I thought for a moment and touched the statue over my heart. *Thanks, God. Thanks a lot.*

I thought of the letter I had written my mother earlier in the evening, and I ran to our mail box. As I was running I was thinking, *How I want that letter back. Now I'll write her a good one.* But it was too late. The mail had been picked up; it was gone. Slowly, I walked back to my bunk. They were playing "Tat-too." It was time to hit the sack. Another long, trying day had come successfully to an end.

As I lay in my sack, the fresh smell of sea air rippled across my face. I inhaled deeply, allowing its special fragrance to digest in my lungs. It smelled so good. I was relaxed. Slowly, my eyes closed, and again I was at peace with the world.

CHAPTER XIII

August 7, 1942, started out like any other training day, except today we would receive our new assignments. And then, in one week—just seven days—we would be leaving Parris Island for home for ten full, wonderful days. A real vacation. Already the excitement was building up. Corr, Pierce, Panos, Setzer, Pinto, and myself had made plans to spend a night in New York. The Great White Way was now dimmed, but all its glory and magic were still there. Corr's father would give us free passes to see the Broadway show *Arsenic and Old Lace*, and afterward we would meet the cast. Then on to Joe Setzer's father's restaurant, The Tomahawk Club, on Fifty-seventh Street. Joe said we would be his guests, and that we would be wined and dined in elegant fashion. To top off the evening, Milo Panos's sister was to be my date for the evening. Her name was Elaine, and Elaine, according to him, was something special—real special. Everything was arranged for the evening of August 20. We would have one big, beautiful bash.

We had just marched in from the boondocks, and although the weather was hot and humid, no one was complaining. It had been a typical training morning. Cpl. Robert E. Howard had put us through all our paces, and we had been marching for the last two hours. We were now returning to our barracks for noonday chow.

From a distance we could see Sergeant Horton standing on the porch of the barracks. He was dressed in full khaki and was carrying his swagger stick. As we marched down the company street, he appeared to be impatient. "Bring 'em up, bring 'em up here," he said. Corporal Howard brought the platoon to a halt. "Left face," he shouted in a military manner. "Order arms. Parade rest." We were now all facing our platoon sergeant.

He hopped down two steps, scanned his troops with his beady, hawkeyed eyes, and proceeded to talk. "At ease, men. I have a few things to say to you. First of all, I want to report some good news. Today, August 7, 1942, the First Marine Division landed on Guadalcanal. The landing was unopposed, and the marines walked ashore. The communiqué went on to say that the marines made contact with the enemy, and that heavy fighting is now in progress. However, the situation is well in hand." A rousing cheer went up from the troops, and then it seemed like everyone was speaking at the same time. "Order—order!" the sergeant demanded. "Knock it off. I'll answer your questions one at a time." Then he pointed to Setzer.

"Where the hell is Guadalcanal, sir?" Everyone was asking the same question.

"Guadalcanal is one of the islands in the Solomon group, located in the South Pacific."

Then another question: "Do you think we will be going there, sir?"

"I can't answer that question for you, but most of you will be seeing action in the near future. I'm sure of that." Then, changing the subject, "Lookie heah, men, I have a lot of things to get finished with. First we'll have mail call." And he proceeded to throw the mail at us in all directions. Some things were never going to change, that's for sure.

After mail call, the sergeant reported that our platoon had to work in the mess hall all next week. "If your name is called out, you're nominated." He then called out forty names. My name was not among them. He called out the head details. Again my name was not mentioned. Finally, the guard duty details, and again my name was omitted. "Okay, men, that's it. After chow, I'll give you your new assignments."

Before he could leave the platform, I ran up to him. "Sir, I'm not on any of your lists for details."

He answered bluntly, "So?"

Awkwardly, I continued, "Sir, I didn't hear my name called."

Raising his eyebrows, he looked annoyed. Looking at him in bewilderment, I just stood there. Answering matter-of-factly, he stated, "You want me to put you on a shit detail, boy?"

Quickly I replied, "No, sir."

Then, looking at me from head to toe, analyzing me with that squinty, icy stare, he exclaimed, "Don't ever question me, boy! Don't ever anticipate the command." Then, still staring me down, his voice grew softer. The calmness sounded like an apology—an apology for all the rotten things he did over the last ten weeks. "I didn't give you any details, boy! There's no mistake. Go join your platoon."

Looking at him squarely in the eye now, he sensed my acceptance when I replied solemnly, "Thank you, sir. Thank you." Swiftly, I left.

After chow, we fell out in front of our barracks. Sergeant Horton appeared. He had an armful of papers. This was the news we were waiting for. He addressed us in a casual manner. "Okay, men, listen carefully for your name and destination."

Assigned to Parris Island for DI training:
Pvt. Edmond E. Scott
Pvt. Robert E. Humpfrey

Assigned to Marine Barracks: Aviation School, Quantico, Va.

Pvt. David Weinberg	Pvt. Michael Shield
Pvt. George Summers	Pvt. Fred Gorsky
Pvt. Carl Johnson	Pvt. Mario Pinto

Assigned to M.B. Portsmouth, Me.
Pvt. Percy Gurney

Assigned to M.B. Washington DC.

Pvt. J. Patrick Monahan	Pvt. Forrest E. Corr
Pvt. Milo Panos	Pvt. Gerard Pierson
Pvt. Henry Summers	Pvt. Vincent Coleman

"The above six men will report to QM School, MB, Hadnot Point, New River, North Carolina. The rest of the platoon will report to Tent City, New River, North Carolina, for advanced training. Okay, men, that's it."

The next few days, the USMC kept us very busy, taking all kinds of government tests, clothing inspections, dress parades, and holding field days. Tuesday we would be leaving the island, so when we had a spare moment we marched to QM areas and turned in our field equipment, rifles, and web gear. Now all we had left was our bedding gear, and we would turn that in the last day.

One day I received a letter from my oldest sister, Lynn. She informed me that she was getting married on August 21, 1942. This came as a surprise to me. I didn't know too much about her future husband, except that he dealt in stocks, bonds, and insurance, and was quite successful. His name was Carlton. I had met him a few times, and he seemed to be a nice guy. Carlton was a well-built man, twenty-eight years old, with jet-black hair combed straight back. He wore expensive clothes and always looked the part of the executive, including the cigar. He was a very forceful and strong-willed man, also very possessive. My sister was the same type of person, plus being domineering. I didn't know whether to send congratulations or condolences. Whichever, the choice was all hers. At least I would attend.

Our training now behind us, we occupied our time playing football, baseball, and volleyball. Sergeant Horton would march us to the athletic field in the morning, and we would participate in intrasquad games. This was a pleasant relief from basic training routine. In a few days, we would be leaving Parris Island, and these games filled in the voids and kept us occupied.

This one particular day, we had been playing baseball for the last two hours. It was a good game, and Joe Setzer had just tied it up with a home run. Sergeant Horton came running onto the field. He was screaming, "Break it up, fall in." He appeared very excited. "Fall in now, goddamnit," he exploded, and we scurried into formation. We never did finish that game, and in no time at all we were on our way back to the barracks. As we marched up the company street, you could see lots of activity taking place. Men were moving in all directions.

"Platoon, halt-one-two. Right face. At ease. Men, listen carefully," he continued. "We were notified by the weather station that tornadoes and twisters are approaching the island. Our job will be to protect the power installations. When I dismiss you, get your water buckets and fall out here on the double." He then dismissed us. In we went and out we came. Then again we fell into two ranks, and Sergeant Horton marched us in double time to the power plant, which was nothing but a long wooden shack. Dismissing us, we stretched out in never-ending single lines. One platoon after another lined up from the sea to the building. Bucket in hand, we formed a bucket brigade. This was archaic. The real fire equipment was at the main area to protect the lily-white asses of the commanding general and his staff. And there we stood, and there we waited, and we waited. We were waiting for an unseen enemy.

The majority of us had never seen a tornado. We had never even seen a twister. However, many of us had read about them in books, and from their description, some of them were devastating. They could uproot trees, tear roofs off of houses, and topple automobiles. They twisted, twirled, and hammered everything in their path. Nothing deterred them from their devilish, wrecking trip. Furthermore, they passed by so quickly in their destructive wake that the proper precaution would be to seek shelter. How the United States Marine Corps, or any rational, sober commanding officer, being of sound mind, could subject his troops to the unpredictable wrath of nature was beyond my comprehension. These pine boxes and orange crates that we lived in and were now protecting were not worth one man's life, but the commanding officer and his staff were risking hundreds of men's lives needlessly. Was it a test of courage? No. Was it a test of valor? No. This was an officer's staff test to prove that men in the Marine Corps were expendable.

From a long distance, we could hear the tornado approaching. The wind was picking up, and the sounds of moaning and groaning were evident. Yes! It was coming, and as it drew closer and closer to the island, the wind was picking up speed, moving and sweeping everything out of its path. I watched the men. I was fascinated by their stoicism; it was admirable. The tornado was bearing right down on us and not one man stirred; not one man moved. Everyone stood their ground. I looked at their eyes. They were big, but there was no panic. They stood there like statues, waiting, just waiting. I took particular note of the anxiety in their eyes and the apprehension on their faces. They were resigned to their fate as a man.

Now no one was talking, but they certainly were praying. I watched their lips and they were moving, moving continually, moving in prayer, as were mine. They were making peace with their Maker, as was I. The tornado was less than a half a mile away. It looked so big, so wild, so high, and ever so black. It twirled and spun like a giant top. Round and round it went, spinning, twisting, turning. It was well over one hundred feet tall, and as it came closer it whistled and it roared. The roar became louder, and louder, and still louder. It was frightening. Like a locomotive it screamed, scaring the hell out of us. Our eyes were as big as saucers now, but still no one moved. It would be upon us in minutes. We dug in and braced ourselves. Then, all of a sudden it veered to the right. So sharply did it turn that it almost split in half. It almost seemed as if God, the DI in the sky, changed his command at the last minute. He heard our prayers.

The tornado continued moving away from us, skirting the island. It followed a straight path into the sea, and we watched as it passed us by. We screamed in delight as it threw water and sand high in the air, and we continued watching until it disappeared in the dark skies. Rain came down in torrents, dispersing the crowd. We slowly made our way back to the barracks. Another day had passed into eternity.

For a while, the tornado was the topic of conversation, and Sunday morning we attended church to give thanks to the Lord for protecting us. The Catholics attended Mass, and the Protestants went to their church services. In our platoon, only two people didn't attend church: Forrest Corr and Milo Panos. Why these men never went to church baffled the rest of us. In our discussions we all agreed God came first, and then country. This was our way of life, and we were proud to display our faith.

Our last Sunday meal on the island was baked ham with sweet potatoes and corn on the cob, topped off with ice cream for dessert. We all agreed that it was the best menu in ten weeks. The rest of the day we spent in recreational games. Everyone was in a relaxed mood.

Monday afternoon, Corporal Howard returned from a five-day furlough. He was in a good mood. Being that we were finished with our

CHAPTER XIV

The last night in our barracks was one of mixed emotions. There was sadness, happiness, and awareness. Because we weren't going home didn't mean the end of the world; we would survive. The majority of us were going to New River, North Carolina, about four hundred miles from here. The first week after we arrived at our new station, we were planning a big bash in the nearest liberty town. We would hire a hall, a band, and lots of food and drink—and most of all, lots of girls, lots and lots of girls. Yes, planning it picked up our spirits. Things wouldn't always be dismal. Despite the war, there would be lots of laughs and many good times. We would live.

Corr, Pierce, Panos, and the two kids were so down in the mouth about not going home that they were planning to go AWOL. I didn't like the idea at all and, acting like a preacher, I told them so. I emphasized that was the last thing they should do. Corr and Panos, the two atheists in our group, said, "Listen to Jesus Christ." I heard their remark but chose to ignore it at this time. The rest of the men also heard it and insisted we drop the subject. It was dropped. Then, again we concentrated on our new home, what it would be like, and the nearest liberty towns. It did sound interesting and most exciting.

Tomorrow would arrive so very fast, and there were two special people that I wanted to see and say good-bye to—Private Monahan and Private Humpfrey. I found Pat Monahan writing a letter to his family. He was just finishing up, and he asked me to wait. Pat wouldn't be going with us. His orders read: Marine Barracks, Headquarters, Washington DC. Now as he approached, I could see that he was still limping. Seeing that I was observing him and feeling a little uncomfortable, he laughed, "Yes, I'm still limping," and then added, "I think I'll be sore for the next two months. I'm sure glad it's over."

"So am I," agreeing with him, but I stated, "I'm sure going to miss some of the people I met here, and you're one of them, Pat." He grabbed my extended hand. I continued talking. "I can't tell you how much I appreciated your friendship, and how very much I enjoyed our topics of conversation. Over the last six weeks, you have made my life on the island so much easier."

Still holding my hand in friendship, he smiled. "Hank," he said, "I was ready to throw in the towel many times. I just couldn't take any more physically; I couldn't take any more, and I didn't have to. I was going home, but when I saw your foot, that one piece of raw flesh, I couldn't believe it. I just couldn't believe that anyone could be so determined to carry on. You inspired me as you did others. I knew then that I could never give up, and I made it." Speaking softly now, he continued, "Hank, wherever you go, God bless you."

"Thank you," I replied, and, squeezing his hand, "Thanks a lot. Good luck to you and yours, and let's keep in touch."

Leaving him, I headed toward Bob Humpfrey's bunk, but he wasn't there. Someone said he was with Sergeant Horton. Then, before I returned to my sack, scuttlebutt (rumor) had it that Bob's father died. No one knew the details. Then, looking up, I spied him leaving the barracks with his luggage. I flew out the door, shouting, "Bob, Bob," and caught him just as he was getting into the jeep. His eyes were red, and the tears in his eyes sparkled like pearls in the soft moonlight. I sensed his feelings immediately, and my own emotions reacted unconsciously. "I'm sorry," I whispered. His mouth opened as if he were going to reply, but no sound came forth. Nodding his head, he gave his approval; he understood. The jeep motor started. Bob looked at me once more, but still words couldn't come. I gently slapped his shoulders. "Good luck, Bob! Thanks for everything." The vehicle pulled away. I glanced at my watch. It was 9:30 p.m.

No sooner was I in the squad room when I noticed Sergeant Horton opening the door of his office. He never came out but stood in the doorway and called to his men to gather around him. They came forward and formed a semicircle around the threshold of the door. Then, in his slow Southern drawl, he told us that he had decided to say good-bye tonight. Standing in the dimly lighted doorway, he appeared as if framed in a picture. He wore a clean, starched khaki shirt that was so salty it appeared almost white. The shirt had fresh-pressed creases running through the centers of his breast pockets, and they appeared so sharp they reminded me of razor blades. His muscular shoulders and V-shaped torso filled out his tapered shirt to such an extent that there wasn't room for a wrinkle. The open collar exposed his bull-like neck, and his sandy hair contrasted his ruddy complexion. The squinty eyes were reflecting the thoughts that were gathering in his mind, and as his thin lips parted in speech, they revealed the whiteness of his sparkling teeth. It's funny I never noticed him in this light before. He was calm, relaxed, and the strain of responsibility seemed to be lifted from his brow. Tonight, he looked handsome. Tonight he looked every inch a marine.

"I want to take this opportunity to wish you all good luck in your new endeavors. At this moment you are trained to the hilt, and if you live to be a hundred years old, you will never forget this training, the Marine Corps, or Parris Island." Then, looking directly at me, he emphasized, "Some of you didn't approve of my practices or my tactics." Here he paused. "But someday soon you'll find them richly rewarding, eminently satisfactory, and wholly convincing." Then continuing, "The will to win has been instilled in you. Always keep that spirit alive. Remember you are marines. Be proud of that fact. Always act like one. Don't degrade the uniform—there is nothing more disgusting than to see a goddamn sloppy-ass marine. Drink moderately, and keep your nose clean. You were a very good platoon and you'll make good marines. Good-bye ... good luck." Then he scanned our faces as if taking one last mental picture. The door closed slowly behind him. Then he was gone, and we knew he wouldn't be back. I thought for a moment. Maybe he wasn't my kind of person, but I couldn't deny in any outfit, he was one hell of a man, a most unforgettable character.

The next morning at 0500 (navy time) we boarded two Greyhound buses. It was very dark, and we groped our way through the blackness onto the bus. Once inside, it was a whole new world. I sank into a soft, cushioned seat next to a window. Joe Setzer sat next to me. I stated, "This is great."

He added elaborately, "This is living."

Yes, this was the nearest thing to comfort that we had known in almost three months. We were enjoying the plushness of the interior, the clean smell, and the soft reading lights. We pushed the handle to Recline and snuggled even deeper into luxury. The bus pulled out.

I sighed as the buses headed toward the mainland, a deep sigh of relief. At last we were leaving this island. I recalled how dark it was when we arrived, and now, how dark it was when we left. Not that it mattered, but I would have preferred to have seen where I'd been. Oh, well! What the hell.

We approached the main gate, and the big vehicles came to a complete stop. Floodlights played on the exterior of the buses. Marine military police snapped to attention as rigidly and as precisely as pistons in a Rolls-Royce, and just as effectively. They examined the bus, the front and the rear, and then the interior, examining every face. After taking the license plate number, they motioned to the driver to proceed.

Once again we continued on our way, and soon we were in the sleepy little town of Yamasee. I recalled the hot afternoon we spent there: the proud storekeeper, and some of the characters we met here. I smiled as I recollected incidents that happened that day. It seemed so long ago, so very long ago.

Once on the highway, the buses' powerful headlights accentuated the blacktop road and the solid white lines. The bus was picking up speed. We were rolling. I looked around. Everyone was either sleeping or reading. It was so very quiet. I enjoyed the solitude. I was content and relaxed with my newfound comfort. My eyes grew heavy, and soon I fell into a peaceful slumber. Washington DC would wait.

CHAPTER XV

"Oh, Dad—buses are anything but comfortable! How awful! That boot camp turned your whole sense of sensibilities upside down!" I said often.

"No, Lisa, really it wasn't that bad. We got used to it. We adjusted accordingly," he answered. "We pretended like we were on the frontier! You know—like Lewis and Clark!"

"What do you mean?"

He started to laugh and continued, "City kids always want to do adventure-related stunts! When your uncle and I were young, we always planned on taking a safari to Africa. Well, we never did get to Africa, so I looked at the war like my adventure time!"

I smiled at his sincerity and caught him getting lost in a memory, the way he so often did.

"Yeah—I'll tell you about one adventure, and an experience that's right up top of any animal encounter I ever heard about!"

I leaned forward and listened.

"Well, honey, let's see, yes! It was 1943. The marines landed on the island of Bougainville on November 1, 1943. It was the biggest of the Solomons and had two active volcanoes. The place was flooded with Japs, thousands of 'em! When the US troops landed, they met a slew of enemies, over forty thousand of them. But they also found a friend. This, Lisa honey, is the story of that friend, my friend, Bougie Sam! So listen up!"

* * *

Life on the island of Bougainville was rough, hard, and unpredictable. The initial landing was a shock. To adapt to your new environment, the transition must start in your mind immediately, and unconsciously with the will to live and survive. Your basic marine training is now applied to tactical operations, and good friends help too. You all share the same problems. "Survival" Their mere presence comforts you, and the conversations strengthen you. We shared likes and dislikes. You need them, and they need you. In combat, they become your brothers.

After a while, life on the island becomes routine. You do things mechanically, almost aimlessly. Nothing seems to matter. Death is all around you. You see it, you smell it, you hear it, but you are prepared for death and are trained to accept the inevitable. Finally, when something good happens, you snap back. It might only be a little thing, but to you, it's a new world. Life becomes meaningful again. You have a new interest; it sustains you. I recall one such incident that brought us back to a normal way of living.

We were working between supply dumps number two and number three. Supply Dump Three had just been established in a place called Evansville. It was practically on the front lines. The jungles were very thick with trees, vines, and bushes. Heavy growth of vegetation was everywhere. Behind every tree or bush you expected to find a Jap or his bullet to find you. It really wasn't so, but your nerves were on edge, and your imagination did the rest. Everyone was tense. When we first landed and someone made a wrong move at night, they were dead.

We took turns doing guard duty. Now in a combat zone, there is no walking post and no one gets out of a foxhole. When you have the duty, you remain awake and keep alert for strange sounds, noises, or movements in the dark jungles. We had at least twenty-five foxholes dug in a staggered line, positioned around the dump. From sundown to sunup, we were on guard in four-hour shifts. During the day, we worked around fourteen hours, carrying everything from ammo to chow. The little sleep we did get, we wanted good protection, and we got it. The charge for sleeping on guard duty in the Marine Corps is a General Court Martial. Marines were responsible people, people you could trust with your life. Cowardice in the Marine Corps is like finding leprosy in New York City. This was the era of "Don't give up the ship." The marines and Seabees on this rock were amazing. They were physical, brave, and courageous, and above all they were spiritually and morally good.

One night Don, Mac, and myself had the guard. I heard a rustling in the trees. Now, it could have been rats or bats or birds, but we had grown accustomed to that kind of noise. This was a big noise. The Japs at times would tie themselves in the trees so they could hang down, after which, during the day when marines would pass, they would open fire with an automatic weapon. Many marines were killed in this manner. My curiosity was aroused, and I knew I shouldn't have, but I did get out of my foxhole. Crawling on my stomach, I made my way to Mac's foxhole about fifty feet away. Lucky for me, Mac wasn't a trigger-happy guy. I circled his foxhole and came up on the far side. I knew he was aware that someone was out there, so when I drew close to his hole, I whispered loudly, "Mac … Mac, it's me, Hank."

Recognizing my voice, he answered softly, "What the hell are you doing out here? I could have killed you!"

I didn't answer him. I was in wet mud up to my ass. "Move over," and I slid into his foxhole. I blurted out, "Do you hear the noises out there? What do you suppose it is?"

"Beats me," he whispered, "but I've been listening to it for over an hour." The time was 0200 (2:00 a.m.). "Should we wake up the men?"

Thinking it over, we decided to wait, because if there were Japs out there, then there couldn't be too many of them. Besides, they had to come to us. Also, the first shot would wake everyone. Besides, the guards on the other side of us must have heard it too.

We waited. In less than ten minutes, three shots rang out. Now everyone was alerted. Periodically an occasional shot was fired into the black forest. Dawn arrived and nothing happened, so we figured the Japs were scared off. Later in the morning we made a search of the area, and there were no signs of Japanese.

The following evening, we doubled our guard and everyone was now on alert. It was raining like hell. The Japs' seventy-seven artillery shells were swishing over our heads. Aside from that, everything was quiet; that is, until around midnight. The same noises we heard the night before returned. Everyone heard it now—it wasn't our imagination. Something was there. A few shots were fired, but again there was no answer.

In the morning, we asked the captain for his permission to search the area. He told us, "If you want to, go ahead, but headquarters reported there is no Jap activity in this immediate area." We left the dump around 0800 with eight men. Johnny, Mac, Don, and myself were in one party. The Nose, Jan, Rock, and Cook were in the other. We figured to walk in a triangle and meet in the middle. This way we wouldn't be separated by any more than a quarter of a mile at any one time. If there was any trouble, we agreed to fire three shots. We said good luck, and with that both groups took off. The jungle became thicker and thicker. Finally, we entered a clearing. It was a beautiful place with not too many trees. Immediately, we spotted something in the tree branches, but it wasn't Japs.

John had a pair of field glasses. He focused his sights on the trees, and proceeded to give us a full account of what he saw. There were animals. He described them. They looked to be the size of a small dog, and they had a face like a rabbit but small ears and large oval eyes. Their tails were similar to a monkey's, and they swung by them as well as a monkey can. They scooted up and down the trees with the greatest of ease. We all took a good look at them and were convinced this was the noise in the night. I counted at least a dozen of them. We became enthused and wanted to capture one; that is, all except Johnny. He was concerned about the other men. "Let's get on with it," he shouted. Reluctantly we left, but I was determined to come back and get one.

We left the area, and in no time at all we were swallowed up in the vast forest. The trees were so high they blocked out the sun, and the vegetation became so thick that we had to machete our way through. It was a slow process but eventually we came into another clearing, and lo and behold we spotted the Nose.

Our friends were very excited. They told us of seeing something most unusual, not too far from where we were. It was a Jap graveyard. We also became excited and wanted to see it. We marched back about a mile, through a swamp that had us in mud up to our ass. We came upon a winding little creek and from a distance, we could see crocodiles sunning themselves on the muddy banks. We avoided them and continued to walk into a broken-down coconut grove. Every tree was sheared off. It was ugly looking. As we continued to walk into the grove, we came upon a sight that I'll never forget. In and among the broken trees were hundreds of dead Japs. This was really the valley of death. These Japs were caught in an artillery barrage, a gift from the Twelfth Marines. So many dead it was unbelievable, but the way they died was something else again. The only comparison that I could make of this scene was to find a park full of wax figures. Some died standing up. Others died in a kneeling or sitting position. Still others took their final breath doing daily chores like cooking rice over a fire, some with cooking gear still in their hands. Most had their eyes open, and they all seemed to be looking directly at us. It was weird, like being in the Twilight Zone.

I often wonder how this could have happened. It was that devastating. I realize it must have been a demolition bombing. I often think of this scene—not willingly, but it's a haunting memory. I ponder the question as to why nobody took cover. I think the bombing came as a surprise. They didn't have a chance. What bothered me was that it was such a waste of young life. Nevertheless, we were carried away with this array of the silent enemy.

Mac stated matter-of-factly, "I hope we meet all our enemies this way." I had to agree. I shared the sentiment.

Another thing that baffled us was that very few of the Japs wore helmets. There were no foxholes and no shelters. There were a few manholes. These were holes with a cover over the top. It was like a manhole cover in a street. Whenever there was an offensive push by the marines, Japs would hide in these holes and let the marines pass over them, and then pick up the lids and shoot a few men. It was a definite form of harassment and was used to demoralize the troops. It was primitive and not very effective. However, it made us aware of the fact that we were fighting a cunning and treacherous bunch of bastards. One could never be too cautious.

After a while, we were having a ball going over this Jap bivouac area. You would have thought that we had just found King Tut's tomb. There were fish heads in wooden tubs. This appetizer didn't make my mouth water, but I did find a can of mandarin oranges and a can of shrimp made for a New York packing house. I quickly put these cans into my pocket. Looking these Japs over carefully, we figured they couldn't have been dead too long, probably no more than thirty hours. The assault troops were moving so fast that they didn't have time to review this spectacle, or maybe they never came this way. The Japs still had their weapons and their personal belongings with them. Normally, advancing troops strip them clean, some even taking the gold fillings out of their mouths. On occasion, the Japs would intentionally leave souvenirs on their dead. They would rig booby traps to the dead bodies, and when marines went to take something off the body, it would explode, sometimes killing them. Today, it seemed like everyone wanted a "memento" to take back home. We weren't any different. In fact, I became so enthused and wrapped up in my new findings that I lost my outfit. It was like turning someone loose at a flea market. I already had two Jap 25 rifles, two 31 rifles, a new Jap dungaree suit, a cap, a helmet, a bayonet, a Jap flag, a bottle of sake, etc. I was going nuts. War does that to you.

The loud noise from the jungle was deafening at times. Birds by the hundreds would screech and beep. They were eating maggots forming on the dead troops' wounds. Flies by the thousands were buzzing all over; not content with the dead, they also wanted the living. Frogs were croaking in every nook and corner of the jungle; flies were their dessert. The artillery firing from sunup to sundown never stopped for one moment, continuous action of the pom-pom guns just adding to the turmoil. Planes overhead dropped their bombs, adding to the noise, and just upped the deafening tempo. It sounded like Forty-second Street on a New Year's Eve.

After a couple of hours passed by, I decided there were enough trinkets to go around to my whole family, relatives, and friends. (What a greedy bastard I turned out to be!) I called out in a loud voice for Mac. No Mac. No Jan. No Nose. Hell: *Nobody!* Here I was alone. Alone. Those lousy bastards just left me. My greed had led me down a blind, timeless path. Looking over the terrain, I didn't realize just how far I had wandered. Everywhere there were dead Japs, Japs, Japs, and more Japs. Many of them had died with their eyes open. It seemed that all of these dead bastards were looking at me. They seemed to be saying, "You'll never get out of here alive, you greedy son of a bitch!" I was embarrassed by my actions. Dead soldiers are still soldiers, no matter what side killed them. I was facing my own end and was ashamed of my behavior.

Quite honestly, the ashamed feeling went by the winds when I hollered aloud, "Up your ass! This is the spoils of war, you bunch of shitheads!" I wandered around aimlessly and became more and more apprehensive. I could see I wasn't going anywhere. I was lost, real lost! Besides being lost, I was also confused. I didn't know the front lines from the back lines, but I had one thing in my favor: I could always talk to God. "God, help me find my way out of this f——king place." When that didn't work, I started to bargain with God. "Please, dear Lord, if I ever get the hell out of here, I solemnly swear I'll never take a damn thing in my life. I know how wrong it is. Please, God, help me get out of here." I prayed continually. I took all the Jap gear and placed it under the heavy foliage. I kept my promise. I never did take another thing. Thinking back now, I bet those items are still buried where I laid them to rest, to this day.

I prayed again for guidance, and my prayers were answered within the next hour. I finally came upon the area where we had found the animals. How greatly relieved I was and how thankful I was for Divine Providence. In no time at all I was back in our camp, amid cheers and boos from my comrades. "We were just going to form a posse and go out and look for you, you stupid bastard!" said the Nose.

"Where the hell did you go?" chorused Rock and Jan. "We screamed our asses off looking for you."

I answered them, "You left me out there to die, you bastards! But St. Anthony** and the good Lord took care of me."

They inquired, "What did you do with the loot?"

"I gave it back to the Japs. No more looting for me. Besides, the shit was all made in Japan anyway!" I slowly walked away. I was starving but it was too late for chow. It was almost nightfall and I was happy to be back. At once I remembered the two cans in my pocket. Hurriedly, I opened them with the help of my bayonet and ate them just as fast. It was delicious. Like a touch of little old New York, little old New Jersey, a little USA! It had been quite a day.

The noises during the night continued to intrigue me more than ever. I wanted to catch one of those womp-cats,* as the natives called them. The Japs took second place in my mind as my curiosity was aroused. Thoughts of capturing this strange animal was becoming an obsession with me. These thoughts were shared by my marine buddies. We set snares, built traps, and made two cages. We tried to lure them into these traps, but it was to no avail. These cats eluded every trap we set. They were uncanny in their movements. Some of these marines had been trapping coons, beavers, and other animals since they were old enough to walk, but they didn't have any luck with these cats. The cats were curious too, because there was evidence that they did examine the traps we set for them.

Determined to get one of these womp-cats, we worked out a plan, a simple plan. First, we would track them and try to isolate one or two in a tree. Once they were treed, and providing it was a small enough tree, we would chop it down. When they ran out, we would grab one in a blanket, tie it up, throw it in a cage, and that would be it. Just as simple as ABC. We built the cages out of corned beef boxes from Argentina. Plans were made, our gear was stored, and now we were ready to go.

I received permission from my commanding officer, Lt. Richard Conway. Now, if there ever was a marine officer who could communicate with the troops, it was this man. His home was Saginaw, Michigan. It's funny, when you're in a combat area, people in general take on a different aspect. You are governed by a special set of rules. You become closer to each other. Life becomes more meaningful. Understanding is the key to better living, and although rank is important, in combat it doesn't seem that important. You call people by their first names. Everything is more on a "buddy-buddy status." In this wretched environment, where life can be snuffed out in less than a minute, life becomes easier and people are friendlier than in civilization. Why is it this way? Why can't people live and let live? Lieutenant Conway was enthused and wished us luck, but he doubted that we would capture anything. I bet him a cherry pie that we would. "Where are you going to get a cherry pie?" he shot back.

"That's your worry, Lieutenant; I'll come back with a womp-cat!" I snickered.

Next morning after chow, we took off on a cat hunt. Five marines came with me: Cook, Maclain, Crane, Jankus, and Derrick. We went to the area where we had seen them before (and where we thought they would be), but there were none to be found. Why is it that when you want to find something, it is never there? We continued into virgin territory about a mile from our camp. It was amazing how fast you got swallowed up in that jungle. The trees were as thick as crabgrass. Vines twisted around huge, thick tree branches. These branches bound themselves around the trunks of bigger trees, creating a mass of vegetation almost impossible to penetrate. We thrashed through with our machetes where we could, and actually had to chop and hack through vines and twines as thick as a man's arm. In some places, we had to use axes to get through. We weren't moving very fast. The trees were a hundred feet tall and in some places the sun's rays were blotted out entirely. From living in these jungles for the past three weeks, we looked pale like ghosts, but yellow ghosts. The Atabrane pills that we took every day to arrest malaria had changed the pigment of our skin from white to yellow. Our faces were as Oriental-looking as any Jap on the island.

We became conscious that we were in wild territory, and we were on the alert for Jap patrols. I used to dream of these things when I was a kid, and how I wished I had lived in the days of the wild and wooly west with all its Indians. Well, this was the nearest thing to it, and despite the dangers, I did find it exciting.

After an hour of most difficult traveling, we came into a clearing. It was beautiful, comparable to strolling through the park on a summer day. The trees were not nearly as tall, or the foliage as thick as in the jungles. This beautiful terrain was covered with tall grass, and you knew that could be treacherous! Sergeant Maclain made us aware not to take chances, and we heeded his advice. He scanned the area with his binoculars, and spotted a clearing where the sun shone through and the trees were sparse. Looking closely, he noted there was activity in the trees and recognized the tree dwellers, known as womp-cats. In fact, he had one right in focus. We all took turns looking at them. We estimated that there were at least ten of them. They were frolicking up and down the trees. They weren't aware that we were spying on them, or perhaps at this distance they felt no threat.

From our observations, as we had seen before, they seemed to be as large as a medium-size dog. Their face resembled a rabbit but with short ears. Their fur was the color of a wild rabbit, and their eyes were large and oval. They had long tails and utilized them just as a monkey would. They could wrap it around the limb of a tree and swing to and fro. They also had long, sharp claws and could climb a tree in seconds. Their teeth were also long and sharp, as we watched them snap branches like matchsticks from safe distance. Some were eating and others frolicking. They were interesting to watch and quite amusing for their private audience.

Don Crane thought we should leave them alone, and I was inclined to agree with him. Derrick, a Pennsylvania trapper of animals including bobcats, also said he had second thoughts about catching one. He said, "It might be like capturing a bobcat: someone's liable to get their eyes taken out or their fingers bitten off."

Cook, from Texas, was insistent. "This is what we came here for, and that's what we're going to do."

Sergeant Maclain chimed in, "Okay, men, that's it! Let's get it over with!" With this remark we moved toward the animals. At least we would try.

As we approached the cats, they scurried and scampered up the trees. They watched us from a safe distance. But they did not appear to be afraid of us. They jumped, climbed, and swung on branches by their tails. They were putting on an exhibition. Indeed, they were fascinating and fun to see. Upright or upside down, they were different.

We figured that we had to begin somewhere, so to disorganize them, we started by throwing stones. This idea just made them climb higher, and they seemed to be laughing at us. Cook suggested that we shoot one down. Back on the canal, we captured parrots this way. We would shoot them in the wing; and when they fell down, we would take them to sick bay, and the corpsman would put a small cast on the wing. In no time at all, they were as good as new and we had a pet. With this type of animal, I said, "No, that would be the last resort."

Suddenly we got a break. One of the cats missed his jump and fell to the ground about a hundred feet from us. We were after him in a second and cut off his exit. He ran for the open fields. He could run, but so could Derrick. Derrick was gaining on him now, and there was one isolated tree, and the cat was running for it. In a flash, the cat jumped for the tree and simultaneously Derrick jumped for the cat. The cat won. He scampered up above and just kept climbing. We watched as he looked at us below, and as he caught his breath, he seemed to be giving us the razzberries. The tree he was in was around fifty feet high, yet it was a skinny-looking tree, with a trunk no more than a foot and a half in diameter. Maclain climbed the tree and tied two ropes on the branches, and two more ropes on each side of the tree trunk. Our plan was to shake the tree so violently as to make the cat jump out of the tree. Two men with the blankets would throw them over the cat, and we would hog-tie the animal and put him in the cage. It was so simple and easy that an hour later that cat was still safe in the tree. We had shaken the tree so violently that we had the branches to the ground, but no womp-cat.

Sergeant Maclain was the lightest, and volunteered to go up in the tree to get him. Jankus handed him a twenty-foot pole and up the tree went Mac. Higher and higher he climbed, but that cat managed to stay five feet away from him at all times. Once or twice, we thought Mac would fall out of the tree, but he always managed to grab onto a branch in the nick of time. "Come on down, Mac!" I shouted. "We're going to chop the damn tree down!"

Mac jumped out of the tree. "Believe me, that cat just won't be dislodged. He really deserves to be free, so let's pack up and leave."

In the meantime, the other cats were coming closer to us. Whether or not they knew the plight of the cat in the tree, and were coming to his aid, or out of curiosity, they were coming to get a better view. Nonetheless, I was watching a big one from the corner of my eye. He was about twenty-five feet from me, and I had a blanket in my hand. I told Jankus I was going for the cat. He said, "It looks like he's getting ready to attack you; that might be his mate in the tree!"

"Who knows," I answered, "but when I count to three, we'll find out!"

I began counting slowly—one, two, three—and I was off and running. My sudden gesture took him by surprise, but he was cagey. He zigged and he zagged like a halfback looking for a hole in the line. I stayed right with him. Back and forth we went and then sideways. He was toying with me. With a sudden burst of speed, he headed for a clump of trees. He ran in a straight line. I was running as fast as I could and gained five feet on him. It was going to be close. I saw the trees directly in front of me. I had to make my move now. The cat was less than ten feet from freedom, and I was not going to lose him. I was going in for a flying tackle.

Within seconds I was airborne, with the blanket opened wide in my outstretched arms. I flew through the air and came down hard on the hilly ground. Underneath that blanket was my womp-cat, biting, but he wasn't fazing me in the least. I remember hollering, "I got him! I got him!"

My friends were there in no time. Cook threw a rope around him, tying him right up in the wool marine blanket. We shoved him into the cage. The cat was quiet. In fact, the blanket was so still, we thought he was dead. However, dead or alive, we were not about to take the wraps off him until we were back in camp. We prepared to leave immediately. Maclain gathered our gear, and in less than fifteen minutes we were on our way. The remaining cats looked at us in dismay. One of their gang would be missing tonight.

There was a large welcoming committee waiting for us when we returned to our bivouac area. Everyone seemed surprised and excited when we told them that we had captured a cat. "Where is he? Where's the cat? Let's take a look at him. Does he bite? Did he give you any trouble?" And so the questions went on and on. The crowd followed us to the cage, and Cook cut the ropes that bound him. Then Mac pulled the blanket off. He was lying in one heap. "He's dead! He's dead," everyone shouted. "You brought home a dead one! You shot him! You killed him." They were disappointed, and this was their reaction.

At that moment, something moved. Everyone noticed it. It moved again. All eyes were on the cage. The animal stood up and shook himself. You would have thought that Notre Dame had scored a touchdown in the last minute of play by the roar of these marines. They were so happy that the cat was alive, and so were we. Our trip had been a success.

The cat didn't have any time to get lonesome because there was always someone playing with him or talking to him. He was never left alone. After a few days, I put my hand in the cage, and he made no move to bite me. I even touched him and he didn't bite. The fellows were skeptical when I suggested taking him out of the cage. "He'll be gone in two shakes," Mac said.

"Well, I caught him and I'm going to take him out of the cage," I said. I took him out and put a rope around his neck. He bolted and started to climb a tree. I pulled him down and there wasn't any resistance. At this particular time, a group of Seabees came into our dump. They too came over to look at this strange animal. The Seabees really got a kick out of this cat. They wanted to know where we found him, how we got him, etc. After all the questions, they promised to make him a harness with a long chain. With the long chain he would have more freedom, and he could climb trees.

The next day his silver harness arrived with the inscription, "Bougie Sam, the Hep Cat," made by his good friends: the Nineteenth Marines, the pioneers engineers, and Seabees. I put the new harness on him and it fit him to a tee. There was a small, lightweight chain attached to the harness; it was over thirty feet long. He was almost free. Now at least he could get around the area. We staked him near the Company Office, and he greeted everyone who came into the dump.

Later a group of marines made him a small jungle set, and he performed his acrobatics for anyone in the vicinity. He could stand on his head or swing by his tail. Inside of a short time, he had adapted so well to captivity that I would take him on walks with and without the chain. I figured if he wanted to run away, well, then let him. He had no such intentions. In fact, if we walked too far, he wanted me to carry him back. He was like a big baby. He was my cat, and he would seek me out if there were a hundred marines there. He loved the attention he was getting. Every day more and more marines came to view "Bougie Sam." They were sure he was more monkey than cat, just by his playful and funny antics.

During the month that followed, our whole outfit became very attached to this animal. Everyone was concerned about his well-being. Not that we didn't have plenty to do about taking care of our own well-being. There were bombings every day and shellings every night. The condition "Black" was still in effect. (This meant that there could be a Jap invasion.) However, the weather conditions were just out of this world. It poured rain day and night, and living conditions were at its lowest ebb. Mud, mud, and more mud was everywhere. We were continuously wet. Again, our working days grew longer and longer. Because of the difficulties of transporting supplies from the beach area due to the heavy rains, we had to change our mode of transportation. The mud was so deep in the roads that 6x6 trucks could not get through. Tractors were the only vehicle that could move in the mud, and it was a slow process. The mud was almost waist high. We were now working twelve to fourteen hours a day. If it wasn't guard duty, then it was hauling supplies by hand. Important commodities like ammo, chow, and clothing were constantly on the move. After moving it to one place, we would unload it at another, and then supply it in one area and issue it at another. The rain hampered us no end. We were constantly wringing wet.

The Torokina fighter strip had been completed by this time, thanks to the heroic endeavors of the capable Seabees. It was up to the marines to hold this little perimeter against over forty thousand Japs. We knew they were on this island, but they were also bogged down in the mud and they couldn't get too many 77s artillery into position, thank God! The few that they did caused enough harassment, so perhaps the rain was a blessing in disguise. The Japs kept trickling in by the hundreds. They were coming in on the far side of the island by boats, but the marines were containing them.

We were spending more time at our supply dump than in our bivouac area. It was necessary that we have supplies in strategic areas, for if there was a big Jap push and then we would be ready for them. To survive and win, this work was a must. Any army is only as good as its supply line. Despite the cursing and the bitching, all orders were carried out successfully.

We brought our cat to the dump too, and here he would never be lonely. "Bougie" got to meet more and more marines every day. Everyone took to Sam. He was a morale builder and a conversation piece all in one, a crowd pleaser with his bag of tricks.

I would be away most of the day, but when I returned, I'd pay my respects to Sam first. I'd burst out with the song, "Sam, Sam, you made the pants too long." He would look at me with those big round eyes, and I'd pick him up and give him a squeeze. He knew he belonged. Then I'd set him free, and he would follow me around like a dog. The temperament of this animal was terrific too.

Everyone tried to grab his long monkeylike tail, and when they did this, he would turn around in a second! He never bit anyone, yet he could bite. His teeth were razor sharp, and he could snap tree shoots right in half with those teeth. Still, he never used his teeth or claws as a weapon. His good-naturedness was amazing. In the evenings we would play cards by candlelight, and Sam would stick his nose in and out of our foxhole to let us know he was around.

We had a radio jeep in our bivouac area and on nights that it didn't rain, we would gather round in the dark and listen to Tokyo Rose. The code name for our area was "William Jig Teer," and the radio men would report to one another that Tokyo Rose was on the air. No one wanted to miss it. It was a must. Each station would report. It went like this, "Lo Hound Nan, this is William Jig Teer. Come in, over."

"This is Lo Hound Nan. Come in, over."

"Happy hour. Happy hour. Come in, over."

"Reading you loud and clear. This is Lo Hound Nan, over and out."

And so it went from one station to another until all stations were alerted. (Yes, we were all tuned in.) Tokyo Rose would say in the sweetest little voice this side of Japan, "And now we will dedicate our next medley of tunes to the Third Marine Division on Bougainville. Oh, incidentally, fellas, come Christmas morning, do we have a big surprise for you! Let's just see what Santa delivers!" she continued. "So sorry most of you won't be here for New Year's, but don't worry, fellas, your girlfriends will be going out with someone new and you won't be missed. So sorry, fellas! Now on with the music," and the turntable would spin out with

"Stardust," "Yours," "Polkadots and Moonbeams," "Blue Moon," Tommy and Jimmy Dorsey, Glen Miller, Frank Sinatra, and Russ Morgan's theme song, "Does Your Heart Beat for Me." The music would fill the night air. It would reecho softly through the jungle.

Pictures would appear. Thoughts of yesterdays would return so vividly that unconsciously you would find yourself smiling, and Tokyo Rose would come in on one of the songs, "Isn't that nice, fellas? So soft. Now let your girlfriend get comfy with your best friend. Now let's have a little more dreamy music," she whispered. Again your mind and thoughts would drift away. Here in the South Pacific, where the stars hung like lanterns so close to the earth, and the bright moon beamed so majestically over the dark mysterious forest, you were aware of the soft tropical winds drifting overhead. You looked up and projected your train of thoughts on a direct course thousands and thousands of miles away, and it all summed up to one wonderful word: *home*. Yes—home. Would we ever see it again? Would we ever?

Then we would come back to reality, and my friends and I would comment on the show. We appreciated listening to the music. Our views were shared by many. We heard many of Tokyo Rose's broadcasts, and perhaps she was guilty as charged, but I never remember anyone turning her off or walking away. Every marine was listening with both ears. Maybe the marines were sadistic, but we enjoyed her chitter-chatter. We had lots of comments about it, some that brought roars of laughter. Everyone loved her music selections, and we never dwelled on the bad things; we didn't have time. Her program was a temporary relief from this living hell, and to keep mentally healthy, you had to enjoy every little avenue of escape, even if it was forbidden fruit.

Time on Bougainville did not move slowly. Every day was a busy one, and each was filled with unexpected surprising events. Some of them were pleasant, but most of them were horrible, and all of them were for real. If you were looking for adventure, it was here in all shapes and sizes. The battle of Piva Forks had just about broken the back of the organized enemy resistance in the Empress Augusta Bay area. Our beachhead now extended over ten thousand yards inland from Cape Torokina and reached from the Laruma River southeast to beyond the

Piva River. Furthermore, there was no question of our air superiority in the region south of Rabaul. Between November 1 and 20, 558 enemy aircraft had been shot down, and the Japanese had only one serviceable airfield left in the Solomons.

The Torokina fighter strip had been completed by this time, and Pappy Boyinton's Black Sheep Squadron was there. To the marines, Pappy Boyinton was a hero and we wanted to see him perform. I didn't miss too many sights on this rock. We were there to see them come in with their victory belly rolls over the airport before they landed. We enjoyed the show immensely. We were also on hand to see the first white woman to land on Bougainville. The papers played it up big, but the nurse just stayed in the cargo plane with its doors open while the movie cameras were grinding away. I don't think she ever put a foot on the soil!

One of the first consignments of cargo to be flown into the Empress Augusta Bay area consisted of fresh turkey for all hands in the division. This arrived on the day before Thanksgiving while the battle of Piva Forks was under way. It constituted practically the first fresh provisions the division had received since landing. The turkey was distributed throughout the division and prepared in every conceivable manner, from being roasted over open fires to being boiled in GI cans. Some units had their turkey immediately upon coming out of combat, while others were fed turkey on their battle positions. Since there was no refrigeration facilities, it had to be eaten as soon as possible after being received. By this time, the division bakery sections were up and functioning, and the turkey was accompanied by fresh rolls. Despite the fact they were involved in the middle of an operation, the men of the Third Marine Division were able to celebrate Thanksgiving in something resembling the customary manner.

At this time of the year, the holiday brought back memories. Thanksgiving on Bougainville was a dismal, cold, damp, rainy day. We had been all over the island that day delivering supplies. We got back to our camp around six-thirty in the evening. I was cold and wet, but mess sergeant Ken Samm didn't forget us. Our turkey dinner was there waiting for us. I put the contents in my mess gear and found a nice quiet spot. A box was my table and my poncho was my chair. The rain had stopped, but it was wet. However, I kept my record intact; I had my turkey leg. Everything was delicious! Really, it was very good. I sat there drinking coffee and looking out into the black forest. My mind started to wander. I couldn't help but think of other Thanksgivings. This was such an important day when I was growing up. Yes, I had such vivid memories.

Looking at that dark background in front of me, I played my little game. I'd see my grandmother and my mother in the kitchen preparing the Thanksgiving dinner. The smiles and the laughter, the hustling and the bustling. All that love going into preparing the feast. I could visualize everyone sitting around the dining room table. The white tablecloth caught my eye. The table was just alive with sparkling glasses and glittering china dinnerware. Smiles and laughter abounded. I could see my father just sitting there, watching my grandfather carving the turkey. My sisters and brother were also watching the operation intently, anticipating what piece they would get. I knew I would be getting the leg. I'd look up at the Tiffany lamp, and then my eyes would catch those starched white curtains and there I'd hold it! That one last look. I would snap back to reality, and believe it or not I'd feel refreshed. True, yes; life was just a game.

Thanksgiving passed quickly, and Christmas was upon us in no time at all. Many new things had taken place. We had established a new supply dump at Evansville. We were closer to the front lines. It is of interest that this dump was actually established and in operation ahead of the advancing infantry regiments, before the Battle of Hellzappin Ridge. Supplies were initially moved into this dump by amphibian tractor. How well I know. I was on that tractor when we delivered twenty-one boxes of K rations and twenty-one boxes of C rations. I was told by Captain Cantella to guard these rations. I spent one unforgettable, scary night alone in this miserable godforsaken place, but that's a story in itself (see chapter I).

On December 25, Christmas morning, we were awakened very early. It wasn't planned that way; it just happened. I remember being in a deep sleep. I awoke in a startling manner. People were hollering and screaming all around me. My eyes quickly opened but it was a dark, still night. It wasn't quite 5:00 a.m. because I remembered checking my watch. Suddenly, something started to happen. My foxhole started to sway in a rocking-cradle manner. The pace quickened, and it was shaking violently! It was so weird! I sat up, startled, and I became apprehensive. I reached for my shoes, my rifle, and all the while I was swaying to and fro. There in the dim morning light, I saw and heard a tree fall down. It fell not too far from my foxhole. The branches and leaves covered a couple of my buddies' foxholes and I could hear them hollering, not in pain, but in fright. In the distance, you could hear the crunching sound of other trees as they fell all around us. My mind was working all the time, and I thought of Tokyo Rose's message of a week ago: "The marines on Bougainville are due for a surprise come Christmas morn." What kind of a secret weapon was this?

Then I heard a distant shout: "It's an earthquake! An earthquake! Earthquake!"

I leaped out of my foxhole and thought to myself, "What the hell do you do in an earthquake?" I was actually swaying with the earth. It was unreal and it made you lightheaded. I made my way to the main area and most of my friends were there. They too were befuddled as I repeated the same sentence: "What do you do in an earthquake?" Bougie Sam had the answer—you just swing in the tree.

The tremors continued for a little while, and then it was just routine. Christmas was just another working day, but we did have a lot to be thankful for. It was my second Christmas away from home, and I was alive and kicking. Perhaps next year I'd be home, perhaps.

The earthquake tremors continued for about a week, but after the initial one they didn't seem to faze us at all. On this island, there were two active volcanoes. Maybe the next excitement would be when they would erupt. This was some rock: over 150 miles long, and two frowns and a snarl wide!

By the New Year, our mission on this island was just about over. The army was taking over, and all lines were being secured. Every passing day found more marines being replaced by army personnel. We couldn't believe the equipment that they were bringing to this island. The Long Toms amazed us. They were long, and they looked like they could shoot across the Pacific Ocean. There were still over forty thousand Japs on this island and after we left, the army needed all the equipment they had just to hold this rock. In fact, the fighting became so bad that the marines were almost called back.

While the marines were on Bougainville, the Japanese lost over 6,000 men and marine losses were less than one-tenth of that number. The Third Marine Division had buried 2,100 Japanese dead. It was so difficult to get our own men into a decent burial ground that, "Who the hell could worry about these dead Japs?" These Japanese were responsible for the rape of Nangking. Just living on this island was a punishment, for it was a living hellhole. I can't remember seeing ten prisoners of war. In fact, I don't know how many Japs survived. Marine intelligence could not have interrogated too many. Custer called the Indians savages because of their brutality. Sherman said, "War is hell." Well, if they were on Bougainville during the last two months, I don't know how they would classify the marines! There was so much hatred for these Japs that if the government went back to the island today, they would find thousands of dead Nips' bones imbedded in old roads. An order came out during the month of December to bury the dead Japanese. Most of them were buried in the highways. The 6x6 trucks, tanks, tractors, and other vehicles ground them right into the roads.

Each morning tractors would come down the muddy, swampy roads carrying our own dead from the night before. Often I would ride down to the beach on one of these vehicles. We would be squatting on the sides of the tractor, and we would be looking down on our dead marines. Some of them would only be dead a few hours and already their faces were turning black. There were at least twenty dead in a truck, and the majority of them were thrown in the truck because the stench was unbearable. Before we would reach the beach, we would have thrown up a couple of times. I recognized some of the faces, especially the mail carrier who would pick up the mail at the beach, and walk it back to the troops near the front. I had walked with this man many times, and we had been shot at often, but the bullets would fall harmlessly in the mud. We never saw the shooter and put it down as stray bullets. However, this is how he met his end, according to the men on the truck who picked him up. I felt sad. Everyone was so young.

It was on one of these trips that I recognized Steve, the marine I had spent the night with at Evansville. I never really knew him, but he had a lot of guts. He was sprawled out on the top of the heap. He had a hole in his forehead about the size of a half-dollar. I asked the driver where they found him. He replied, "Not too far from the Evansville Dump, and he must have been dead a week." I told him two weeks, to be exact. It was now November 28. I thought he might have gotten away that night. Well, I could be lying there next to him. I stepped down and walked across the bodies to Steve to look at his dog tags. I saw the chain and I tried to pull it out. I lost my balance. I touched his head and I got sick. I heaved my guts up. We were at the beach.

We received notification from headquarters that we would be leaving Bougainville on January 9 for our home base on Guadalcanal. I could have gone back to the canal two weeks earlier when my outfit, the Ninth Marines, were relieved by the 164th Army Infantry Regiment. Instead, I asked my commanding officer, Captain Cantella, for permission to stay with the division. I had a lot of friends in the division, and the rough part was over. I certainly would never miss this island, with its constant rain, mud, Japs, crocs, earthquakes, live volcanoes, malaria-carrying mosquitoes, pesky insects, flies, scorpions, rats, land crabs, treacherous surf, etc., but I would miss our womp-cat. We had decided when we first caught Sam that if and when we left the island, we would release him in the area where we had found him.

Early on the morning of January 8, 1944, Mac, Don, and myself took Sam for his last walk and released him in haunts that were familiar to him. When we arrived at the area, there were a few of his friends scampering around, and with his personality we just knew he would adjust in jig time. We were a little sad to see him go, for he had become a part of our life on this rock. He was the bright spot in a rather dull, miserable existence. Sam, indeed, had brought us a lot of pleasure. We would never forget him. When we released him at first he stayed right with us, but after fifteen minutes of roaming around, he occupied himself in the area and we quietly stole away.

The remainder of the morning was utilized in packing our gear, writing letters, and saying good-bye to old and new friends, wishing them luck and hoping that we would see them in the near future. Rocky came up with the bright idea that we should go to Evansville. Yes! Evansville, where we had established a supply dump many, many weeks ago. According to Rocky, Sergeant Norakowsky and Charlie Severe were running the dump. These men were some of our closest friends. Rocky kept ranting, "Come on, let's go up there and give the Big Polack the heat! Come on! There's nothing doing here! Come on! The Rooster [Jim Seals] and all the rebels are there. Let's have some fun, come on, get off your ass! Let's go." So it went on and on. Finally, five of us decided to go with him.

We arrived in Evansville at 1500 navy time (3:00 p.m.). The place had certainly changed, and all for the better. My mind wandered back to the first day that I saw this place. "My God! What a night!" I thought, and then I shook it from my mind. It did shape up well. They even had a mess hall, such as it was. The fellows were so happy to see us. We were amazed by their hospitality. Even the rebels broke out the raisin jack and the cherry jack, and if that wasn't enough, then 190-proof white lightning cut with grapefruit juice would certainly wet your whistle. They were pulling out all the stops. The laughs were becoming contagious, and the tales were great. We were enjoying their company and their chatter immensely, so much so, that we decided to stay for chow. We were glad that we came. It had been fun and Rocky was right, "We would have a good time." The sergeant in charge of the mess hall baked us a Spam dinner. Spam with pineapple rings on top was on the menu. He camouflaged it so well that it didn't even taste like Spam. In fact, believe me when I say it was the best meal we had on the island, and it almost turned out to be our last.

We were just finishing our meal. We were having our coffee and leisurely shooting the bull when all hell broke loose. The Japs were lobbing mortar shells all over the place, and we were directly in their line of fire. *Swoosh! Bang! Bam!* The Japs were shooting the shit out of this place. We didn't hang around long enough to see the damage. We flew out and jumped into the nearest foxhole. Mortar fire continued periodically throughout the night. Rocky, the good guy who brought us here, now became Rocky the bad guy. All in the short space of two minutes, Rocky went from hero to goat.

The Nose, Noel Breault, was an outspoken person under normal conditions. This situation aggravated him more so. He called Rocky every name in the book, from shithead to lard-ass. He had a way with words, some of it not fit to print. He did say, "If it wasn't for your stupid suggestion to come here, we would now be relaxing on the beach, just hanging around, shooting the bull and waiting for our ship to come in. Now we will probably all get killed, and we can all thank you, lard-ass."

Rocky was a big lovable guy who kind of reminded you of a big St. Bernard dog. He bore the brunt of many of our outbursts, but he took it all in stride, and many times he had the last word. His famous words to me were always, "I'll take care of all your girlfriends."

Finally, the long night passed and so did the harassing mortar fire. We said our good-byes and caught the first truck out of the supply dump. When we arrived back in our bivouac area, everyone was already packed and raring to go. I received the good news from Sgt. John Roth that I had been promoted to buck sergeant. This meant that I would buy cigars for all the men in our outfit. In return, all my friends would tack on my stripes (they would punch my arms black and blue).

Before we left camp, we had a problem. Bougie Sam came back home and he was in rare form. It didn't take him long to spot me, and you would have thought I hadn't seen him in a year. He knew something was up, and he wouldn't leave my side. We didn't have time to take him back to the area where we had found him, so by his favorite tree we piled food and figured he would stay there, but nothing could induce him to stay. He wanted to be with the gang.

Orders came to fall in. We had our last muster before leaving for the beach. Sergeant Casey called roll call, and we started our last march to Torokina Beach. Looking back in retrospect, we were a sad-looking bunch of marines, but our spirits were very high. We were happy to leave, and we sang songs all along the way. One of our favorites was the "Raggedy-Ass Marines Are on Parade."

After a while, everyone seemed to grow quiet and their faces somber, as we trudged along the muddy road filled with tractor and tank marks. Sam the Cat kept close to me. Every once in a while, he would brush up against me, and then look up at me with a questioning stare with those big round eyes.

We finally arrived at the beach and it was beastly hot. The sun was riding high, and the sand was commencing to boil. Despite the heat, there was a strong wind blowing inward from the ocean. This breeze gave us some relief, and at times it was refreshing. From being in the jungle for the last couple of months, we had forgotten how bright the tropical sun really was. Our eyes squinted from its powerful rays. The sun's reflection on the waters of Empress Augusta Bay made it difficult to see the ships anchored at least a mile out in the bay. At that distance, they looked like toys. The ship that would sail us back to Guadalcanal, our home base, was the USS *President Jackson*. It was one of the ships of the presidential line and was considered a good troop ship.

The beach itself was jam-packed with men, gear, and vehicles. Again, looking back in retrospect, I often compare this scene with the Bible history story of the building of the Tower of Babel, a city where men tried to build a tower to reach heaven. They were stopped by God, who caused them to speak in different languages and scattered them over the earth. Well, this was the scene. Bullhorns were blaring, trucks were honking, cranes were grinding, brakes were screeching, and sergeants screaming orders added to the noise and confusion. It was a place of bedlam. However, in due time we grew accustomed to the noise. We tried to make ourselves comfortable. We were waiting for embarkation directions and it was most difficult, for bullhorns were blasting in all directions. "Now hear this. Now hear that." After an hour of listening, we finally heard the announcement that pertained to our outfit. "Now hear this: Marines, prepare to embark on Red Beach." Again and again, they screamed, "Marines, prepare to embark on Red Beach!" The marines acknowledged their approval with a deafening roar, and slowly we marched to the Red Beach embarkation station.

Poor Sam all this time was in such discomfort. The noise and confusion had him scared half to death. Despite all the ruckus, however, he stuck close to me as glue. I wondered, *What am I going to do with him? He can't come back to the Canal. First of all, it isn't fair to him. Second, he might not adapt. And last, the worst reason of all: the US Navy does not allow pets aboard ships!"* I thought anxiously.

We took him to the edge of the jungle three times in a row, and each time he made his way back to the beach. We hollered, "Scat, Cat! Get lost!" Nothing could deter that animal's spirit. He was so determined to be with us. Time was of the essence. Our group was the next up to enter a Higgins boat. Quickly, I took the rope from my pack and grabbed Sam and ran into the jungle. I tied him to one of the trees, explaining at the same time to Sam just why he couldn't come with us. I figured sooner or later someone would find him and set him free, or better still, adopt him as a pet. Eventually, he would forget us. Again, I bid him good-bye and ran back to my outfit as fast as I could.

We lined up for the Higgins boat. The sea was exceptionally rough. Whitecaps were forming all over the water, and a stiff breeze was blowing. It was now 1300 navy time (1:00 p.m.). We entered the Higgins boat with our seventy-five-pound transport packs strapped to our backs, and our M1 rifles slung over our shoulders. In a minute we would be on our way. Then on the ramp of the Higgins boat, there was a big commotion. I quickly saw who was causing it. Bougie Sam jumped aboard, amid the cheers of the marines on the land and on the sea. Nosing his way through the crowd, he came right up to me. There wasn't anything I could do now, so I bent down and held him close.

The loading ramp of the Higgins boat was slowly being raised. It was raising like a drawbridge over a castle moat. It slowly, ever so slowly, closed and then, with a bang, it clamped shut. The grinding gears were suddenly quiet, and only the powerful idling sound of the motor remained. Suddenly, the engine roared and we slowly backed away from the island shore. As we drew away from the shoreline I took one long, sweeping look. With my last glimpse of the island, I reflected on the history that was made here. I thought to myself, *How many people will remember this island five years from now?* I knew that I would never forget it. Never.

It was then I spotted the American flag. A funny thing about the American flag: no matter where you fly it, it always appears to be in the right place. Gazing over the horizon, I had never seen it appear so magnificently and significantly displayed, as when I was leaving the island of Bougainville. Underneath that beautiful flying flag were hundreds and hundreds of little white crosses. They marked the gravesites of the US Marines who paid the supreme sacrifice. They, too, had dreams for the future. So young and all so brave, but their dreams came to an end, here, like a sudden stop. It was all over. They died for our country, for your and my freedom, and for this flag. "There's a Star-Spangled Banner Waving Somewhere" was a very popular song at this time. Well, this island was that "somewhere."

Our boat now spun around in a semicircle, and finally we headed for the open sea. In the distance our ship loomed like a toy. It was so far from land. No one was talking now. Everyone seemed in a pensive mood. The coxswain had the throttle wide open as we headed for the open sea. The boat zoomed through the rough surf, bucking like a bronco. Up and down, over the swells, and in and out the whitecaps. The boat continued on its erratic course, continually spraying a steady, misty stream of salt water into the boat. Every once in a while, a full wave would break against the bulkhead, swamping the boat with water and splashing down on the marines. We were soaked to the skin, and the bleak wind just added to our discomfort.

I had been keeping a sharp eye on our cat, and Sam's discomfort was very much apparent. He did not take too kindly to the salt water. I removed my jacket and wrapped it around him. He was shivering, and then he started to shake violently. The sea water and the rough ride were taking its toll. He started to throw up his food. God! God Almighty! Was he seasick! So very, very seasick! I picked him up and cradled him in my arms. I talked to him softly, whispering in his ear, "Everything is going to be all right, Sam." He looked at me with those big round eyes. They seemed to say, "I trust you implicitly." I told Don to get my poncho out of my pack. Carefully I wrapped it around him, and then holding him close to me, he seemed to be perfectly contented; his shivering ceased. Again, I reassured him that everything would be all right.

We approached the USS *President Jackson*, and excitement started to run high as the coxswain maneuvered the Higgins boat into position for embarkation. We were observing the size of this ship. It wasn't exactly the *Queen Mary*, but it sure looked big. The embarkation nets were draped over the starboard side of the ship, and they were fastened to the promenade deck. The ship was riding high in the water. By riding high, I mean that the ship was empty. There was no cargo in the hold. This added at least twenty feet to the height of the ship from the water line. Looking directly up from the Higgins boat to the ship's promenade deck, it compared to be looking up from the street to the top of the Empire State building (of course slightly exaggerated, but it was high). We had a seventy-five-pound transport pack to haul up with us—now, plus a twenty-five-pound womp-cat. It would be quite a haul.

The water had become very choppy now, and the rocking boat was slamming repeatedly against the side of the ship. This continuous motion, combined with the water in the boat, made the footing very slippery and treacherous.

Standing on the first deck of the ship, observing all operations, were the ship's officers. We spotted them immediately as we made our first approach toward the ship. In their clean, starched khaki uniforms and their braided barracks hats, they looked very sharp, but in this combat theater, they appeared out of place. In their hands were bullhorns, and they were shouting orders to the coxswain below. All of a sudden, the embarkation nets dropped into the boat. We could see they were scanning us with binoculars. They immediately spotted Sam. Their horns blared from above, "Get rid of your pets! No animals are allowed aboard this ship." Again and again they repeated the same orders. I still didn't put Sam down, and they screamed, "Get rid of your pet! That's an order from the executive officer!" All the marines were looking up at the officers in silent contempt.

Then one lone voice screamed out from the Higgins boat. "Up your cotton-picking ass! We're coming aboard." The marines grabbed the climbing ropes, screaming and shouting as they scampered up the rope ladders. I held on to Sam and started the long climb with one hand.

Bullhorns were now blasting in all directions. "This is your executive officer speaking, get rid of that animal!"

At this time I was oblivious to their commands. I continued up the ropes with Sam in my arms. We were almost at the promenade deck now, and I could feel a million eyes watching my every move. Navy personnel would be awaiting my arrival. Looking down below, the Higgins boat was still there. The height kind of made me dizzy, but only for a second. The climb was strenuous and tiresome, but it was much easier than I anticipated. My strength returned, and with renewed vigor, I was determined that I would not give my cat up easily.

When I finally reached the top landing, my marine buddies formed a ring around the sailors and officers, separating me from them. No one grabbed me, and no one said anything. Instead, they just stared. They had never seen an animal like Sam before. It was quiet as they looked at me in astonishment while I laid the poncho containing Sam's body on the cold steel deck. Slowly, I pushed back the flap and looked at his eyes. They were closed. Still, no one uttered a word. Then a corpsman with a stethoscope bent down and examined his body. He summed up the situation abruptly and in two words: "He's dead."

A lump came to my throat. I looked up at the marines. They were gazing at Sam, and everyone removed their helmets. It just seemed the right thing to do. Mac and Don bent down and wrapped Sam gently in the poncho, and tied it securely with a tent rope. Then Mac looked up at me like he was waiting to get an approval. Gently, he pushed the body into the sea. We watched it sink into the silent deep.

The crowd dispersed in silence and disappeared into the holds below. The navy had just witnessed another side of these tough marines. They were incredible, but little did they realize that the marines had just lost a friend. A good friend. Bougie Sam would be remembered as the pet who lost his life, wanting so much to be a part of theirs.

EPILOGUE

I sat and cried. With my face buried deep in the muscles behind a Hanes white T-shirt, I sat on my father's lap and wept. I couldn't have been much more than three or four years old, the first time I remember hearing the story of Bougie Sam. My father held me and brushed the hair from my face with his heavy hand. He returned my gaze, always, with a somber expression. "Oh, Daddy!" I cried. "Oh, Daddy, poor Sam! Poor little Sam!"

"Yes," he whispered, "poor Sam. He was so good." My father's arms tightened around me, and for just a moment, he rocked me back and forth. And then he spoke, "Lisa, war is hell. Remember this, my dear little girl: war is hell."

FOOTNOTE

* For decades, the phylum and genus of Dad's pet remained a mystery. Although Bougainville and his adventures during the war were relayed over many a holiday dinner table, any confirmation regarding a creature like "Bougie Sam" eluded us. It wasn't until the year 2008 that we received the missing puzzle piece.

Our friend Suzanne Parmly of Red Bank, New Jersey was hostess to a wonderful celebration honoring Memorial Day. Great cheer and food was had by all. In attendance was a musician and songwriter named "8 Ball Aiken," with his wife Byrd. After mention of my father's military service, the couple seemed to warm up.

8-Ball was actually thanking my Dad for serving and protecting his native country of Australia. He stood up from his chair, extended his hand, and said, "Thank you, sir, and thanks to all of your friends, all the other United States Marines." My father was speechless. He was totally taken aback with this gentleman's display of thanks and gratitude. I could read his face, because, by the year 2008, I knew his face inside and out and up and down. My father wasn't only my sole surviving parent, he was also my best friend. He looked wonderful at that moment. So very humble and gracious, yet bursting with smiles and pride, all in the same breath!

Later on, 8-Ball entertained us with his musical talent. Boy! Did Hank ever love his performance on the guitar. He spoke of what a great time we had at that party for months afterward, and his eyes would shine. He even insisted that I buy all of 8-Ball Aiken's CDs, and send one off to my brother, Hank Jr., out west. He enjoyed him that much.

When the talk turned to the meaning surrounding the holiday and the subject of war (and with Hank, the talk always turned to the subject of war. Of that you could be certain.), "Of course, yes!" the young couple chimed in together. "We certainly have seen such an animal!"

My father froze. His eyes and ears pricked up. He hung on their every word with an uncharacteristic reverence. Aiken went on to say, "Nice face like a rabbit with real big eyes and a long tail like a monkey. He's agile and quick."

"That's him!" shouted my father, jumping right up out of his seat. "That's exactly how he looked!" he nodded, with his finger still pointed in the air and his face flushed red and excited.

"Yes, I've seen them," concluded Aiken. "You described the Australian possum. They live in the trees."

"Ya see!" stammered my father. "Finally!" He sat back down and looked more satisfied than I could ever remember seeing him. It's an interesting phenomenon, how a person's face can change right in front of you when they know that they've broken through some barrier.

Hank was well-pleased. He was grinning from ear to ear with those postwar pearly whites! "Ya see?" he kept on saying. "I knew someone had to know what the hell I was talkin' about!" He was a little breathless and happy. Glancing around the room, however, I wondered if anyone else at that party had any idea of what had just gone down.

** "St. Anthony of Padua was born in 1195 in Lisbon, so the Portuguese claim him. Indeed, in Brazil he is frequently shown garbed as an officer of the army, and the Franciscans in that country draw every year the pay due his rank of general. In Portugal, he was enrolled on January 24, 1688, as a private in the Regiment of Lagos. Five years later, he was promoted to a captaincy as a reward for the miracles he had performed for the troops." (Maynard)

References:

Maynard, Theodore. *Saints for Our Times*. New York: Image Books, 1952.

Original intro, circa 1980s

I graduated high school in 1940. The economy was not very stable, or so it seemed, because the country was easing out of the Depression of the thirties. As each day went by, the industrial areas looked more promising for modest prosperity.

War was raging in Europe, and the supplies our country produced were needed desperately. New factories were opening up and the old ones were operating on two and three shifts. I didn't particularly like factory work, but because of financial need, I was forced to work in one. Soon I was in the blue-collar field and worked in a number of places: a button factory, a paper-box factory, an auto repair shop, as a clerk in a grocery store, a commercial laundry, and in a lamp and electrical factory. Every time I left a job, it was for more money.

Most jobs in 1940 hinged on people you knew or friends of the family. Such an arrangement brought me to work in New York City. The job was only a fair one, and the pay was low, but I was in a white-collar field. Expenses were high and I slowly was starving, but I worked with some of the most wonderful people I ever knew.

The bombing of Pearl Harbor changed my life. During Christmas week, I and two close friends enlisted in the US Marines. The marines in those days were a close-knit outfit with very high physical requirements and stern discipline. I was chosen and with one phone call, my life was changed. The next day, I left for Parris Island.

Boot camp at Parris Island proved to be a nightmare, but despite its shortcomings and hellish experiences, it was a key in the molding of all the men's lives who were there. It more than prepared you for war; it prepared you for life and readied you for death. Men became stoic in their suffering and loneliness, mainly because there was no one to whom you could relate. You couldn't relate to people, and you couldn't communicate. This training took a lot out of you, but it added moral stability and triggered a clear understanding of righteousness.

Four years of war dragged on. By being in the Pacific and other faraway places, I did gain knowledge, and I added more and more virtues to my already long list of character outline, namely tolerance, patience, integrity, and fidelity. The South Sea islands taught me lesson upon lesson. I learned to appreciate the art of unadulterated natural beauty. The colorful hues of the island terrain mingled with the pastel shades of the majestic blue ocean water. A magnificent tropical sky held pillowy white clouds, which drifted aimlessly about in the celestial heavens. Despite the bombings and the smell of death, the natural beauty overcame all.

Even today it enhances my memories, especially those of the graveyards. I never minded graveyards, because my father died when I was six years old. It was our family routine to visit him and have a picnic under the trees in North Arlington Cemetery. It was a place to cherish memories, whether they be of laughter or tears. I felt the same way about the graveyards during the war, because like every other marine, I knew that any one of them, on any given day, could end up being my final place. And to tell you the truth, they were beautiful.

CPSIA information can be obtained at www.ICGtesting.com
Printed in the USA
BVOW071854021211

277432BV00002B/4/P